SAP® Enterprise Performance Management (EPM) Add-In

Kermit Bravo
Scott Cairncross

Kermit Bravo & Scott Cairncross:

SAP® Enterprise Performance Management (EPM) Add-In

ISBN:	978-1502337016
Editor:	Alice Adams
Cover Design:	Philip Esch, Martin Munzel
Cover Photo:	Fotolia: #43547661 © sato
Interior Design:	Johann-Christian Hanke
Layout:	1-2-buch.de, M. Albrecht

All rights reserved.

1st Edition 2014, Gleichen

© 2014 by Espresso Tutorials GmbH

URL: *www.espresso-tutorials.com*

Feedback
We greatly appreciate any kind of feedback you have concerning this book. Please mail us at info@espresso-tutorials.com.

Content

Preface

The objective when we started writing this book was to provide useful information about the SAP EPM Add-in to jumpstart project implementations, facilitate end-user training, and help newcomers leverage our experience in practical manner.

During the course of this book, we will guide the reader through the key concepts and components to build a strong foundation of knowledge in order to more effectively work with the EPM Add-in.

In the first chapter, we discuss how the SAP EPM Add-in came to fruition after seven years of strategic acquisitions by SAP. Chapter 2 introduces a simplified business case for use in subsequent chapters: Rosie's Lemonade Company. The case study is explained in detail and is foundational to the rest of the chapters and examples in the book.

While the example is fictional, real-life scenarios were taken into account in order to deliver value to the reader. By explaining functions and features within the context of a business example, the reader will find the contents of each chapter easier to understand.

It is important to realize that not all tips and tricks will be applicable to every scenario that you will encounter in an implementation. However, this book will give you a good idea of how to approach any challenge.

Target Audience

We wrote this book with a wide audience in mind; it should appeal to different implementation roles ranging from consultants to business users and does not require expert knowledge about SAP (or any experience using the SAP EPM Suite for that matter).

For entry-level and seasoned SAP practitioners alike, this book will serve as a reference guide that distills years of experience and focuses on some of the most frequently used features in successful implementation projects. This book offers tips, tricks, and time savers that can immediately be applied.

Architects and planners can read this book to get a better idea of what the EPM Add-in and BPC is capable of.

For management, this book describes different options for implementing the EPM Add-In; it can be used to make informed decisions before committing to a project.

Finally, business users can continually reference this book to learn new functionality, as well as strengthen core concepts and facilitate the communication amongst different teams.

Introduction to the content

Readers can expect to learn about the key features and concepts that the EPM Add-in brings to the table.

The reporting process is covered in detail and we will outline simple practices that will make report building, support, and maintenance easier.

This book talks about the main functions and features that can be used to format a report and how simple tweaks can make a big difference in creating corporate templates for branding.

Report builders and planners will learn how to create input schedules in much the same way as creating a report. In addition, we explore key EPM settings that control how reports behave and display.

Data manager packages are also explained in detail. Both basic and advanced features will be covered.

The book also gets into troubleshooting techniques, common errors, and monitoring features available to give a primer for newcomers on where to start looking in order to get past frequently faced issues.

The reader can also expect to learn a little bit about advanced functionality such as working with EPM-related Visual Basic for Applications macros, SAP BusinessObjects Dashboards, and the SAP EPM Excel Ribbon.

Acknowledgements

We would like to thank all the people that participated in the production of this book. Their advice, contributions and help have helped in the realization of this book.

We would like to offer thanks and special appreciation to the following people:

- ▶ Alice Adams at Espresso Tutorials, editor of this book, for her assistance, patience, and guidance through the entire process of creating this book.

- ▶ Martin Munzel at Espresso Tutorials, for his assistance and support from the early stages of approving the outline through the completion of the book.

- ▶ William Chuang at TruQua Enterprises, who helped during the review process of the first three chapters of the book and provided valuable feedback that has been incorporated into this edition.

How to work with this book

This book is divided into six consecutive chapters plus an outlook chapter, the first four of which take you through the basics of SAP HANA and will lead to practical finance and controlling examples. Chapters 5 and 6 explain in details the latest developments made by SAP, such as SAP Collections Insight, SAP Working Capital Analytics or Financials Add-on for SAP Business Suite powered by SAP HANA.

In the text, boxes are used to highlight important information. Each box also has an icon to identify it more precisely:

Notes offer practical tips for dealing with the respective topic.

Examples illustrate a topic more clearly.

Warnings draw your attention to possible sources of error or stumbling blocks in connection with a topic.

Go to the homepage of Espresso Tutorials to watch a video.

Finally, a note concerning the copyright: All screenshots printed in this book are the copyright of SAP AG. All rights are reserved by SAP AG. Copyright pertains to all SAP images in this publication. For simplification, we will not mention this specifically underneath every screenshot.

1. About the EPM Add-in

1.1 Overview

The Enterprise Performance Management or EPM Add-in for Microsoft Office was released as a unified Excel-based frontend for the SAP EPM 10.0 Suite. The EPM Add-in was built in order to harmonize a number of Microsoft Office based clients used within the SAP BusinessObjects and EPM portfolio. This tool contains the best of all of the products it unifies, which enables a vast array of features and functions that provide business users rapid time to value.

1.1.1 SAP acquisitions in the analytics space

From 2007 through 2010, SAP acquired a number of companies that make up its analytics portfolio today. OutlookSoft, Pilot Software, and Business Objects are just a few of the key acquisitions that embody the core of SAP Analytics today. As a result, SAP inherited a number of different Microsoft Office-based tools in addition to its own that had varying strengths and weaknesses. For example, SAP acquired Business Objects who previously acquired Cartesis and ALG Software that eventually became their Financial Consolidation and Profitability and Cost Management solutions, respectively. Each of these products had their own front-end tools and functionality that was merged into the EPM Add-in for Microsoft Office. As a result, the EPM Add-in incorporates a lot of the functionality from the older tools, in particular deriving a lot of the "look and feel" from Extended Analytics Analyzer that was part of Cartesis.

The EPM Add-in is now much more standardized and integrated across SAP and non-SAP applications and technologies, as enterprise customers would expect from a mega-vendor like SAP. Integration and interoperability extends beyond the EPM Add-in, from support of the EPM suite of applications into the SAP Business Suite including but not limited to ERP, CRM, and SCM. Post-acquisitions, SAP BPC version 10.x embodies the level of integration across applications and technologies that has always differentiated SAP.

After the acquisition of SAP BusinessObjects in 2008, SAP shuffled around the products that make up the EPM Suite. SAP went through a rigorous process to choose not only the best products, but also those with the highest potential for adoption. The matrix below highlights each product selected within the core subject areas that make up the EPM Suite.

Product Space	Product Name	Product Information
Strategy Management	SAP Strategy Management (SM)	Formerly Pilot Software. Application to help visualize strategy and tie strategy to execution.

Profitability / Cost Allocations	SAP Profitability & Cost Management (PCM)	Formerly ALG Software, acquired by BusinessObjects. The product was originally developed with a much broader target market, however there were already other products in SAP covering these areas.
Planning Budgeting & Forecasting	SAP Business Planning & Consolidations, version for SAP NetWeaver (BPC NW) SAP Business Planning & Consolidation, version for the Microsoft Platform (BPC MS)	Formerly OutlookSoft. Although this product was originally developed for the Microsoft Platform (the SQL Server Suite), a year and a half after the acquisition of OutlookSoft a sibling product was released on SAP's native NetWeaver platform, which is accelerated today with the use of SAP HANA.

Consolidation	SAP Business Planning & Consolidations, version for SAP NetWeaver (BPC NW) SAP Business Planning & Consolidation, version for the Microsoft Platform (BPC MS) SAP Financial Consolidations SAP Business Consolidations (BCS)	As the name suggests, consolidations is a big part of BPC and one of the core reasons why SAP bought OutlookSoft. A unified forecasting and consolidations platform is a core strength of the BPC offering which resonated well with the market and continues to do so today. Within Europe, where complex consolidations scenarios are the rule versus the exception, there were two different products which filled this niche: Financial Consolidations and SAP BCS. BCS had been a part of the suite preceding EPM, SEM and had gained some traction so that development to support legal updates was continued.

		Financial Consolidations, formerly Cartesis, is very good at handling distributed and complex consolidation scenarios and had, like BCS, gained a lot of traction so it too coexisted in this space.

In 2009 during the launch of the first full versions of many of the products within the SAP EPM portfolio, there were Microsoft Office clients for:

▶ SAP Business Planning & Consolidation (BPC) 7.5, version for SAP NetWeaver

▶ SAP Business Planning & Consolidation (BPC) 7.5, version for the Microsoft Platform

▶ SAP Profitability & Cost Management (PCM) 7.5

▶ SAP Financial Consolidations 7.5

In addition to the tools noted above, there were products that had tools that also integrated with EPM and Microsoft Office that became superfluous. Other competing Microsoft Office-based front-end clients were designed for other business intelligence purposes and integrated with EPM data only as an afterthought for marketing purposes, while others were kept for legacy purposes to satisfy customers comfortable with the pre-existing options. A few of the earlier options that persisted included:

- ► EPM Extended Analyzer

- ► SAP Analysis, for Microsoft Office (formerly Pioneer)

- ► SAP Business Explorer (BEx) Analyzer

At the end of the day, there are still a number of products for SAP customers to choose from, as well as a smorgasbord of Microsoft Office clients for SAP to maintain and support.

When discussions surrounding the EPM 10.0 Suite first began, they centered on what the foundational themes of the suite should be. The three key themes of the product suite were:

1. Connect – Another way of saying integration. SAP was focused on providing deeper integration within the EPM suite, as well as with additional SAP portfolio products such as SAP ERP, SAP BW, and the SAP NetWeaver Portal.

2. Extend – Although SAP turned laser focus to integration, SAP wanted to remove the seams between the products in the suite to ensure that 10.0 was best in class. In order to ensure that each product within the suite continued to be best of breed, SAP also incorporated additional features and functions requested by customers and partners into the release.

3. Harmonize – A new web interface along with common standards made up core aspects of the harmonization theme. In addition to these standards, SAP planned to develop a common Microsoft Office client across all of the products within the product suite.

This client contained all of the best aspects of the various clients within the SAP portfolio and modernized the end-user experience, thereby taking the EPM Suite to the next level: the EPM Add-in (see Figure 1.1).

Figure 1.1: The EPM Add-in for Microsoft Office

1.2   The connection concept

Creating a tool that can connect or consume information from large quantities of data repositories is challenging. One of those core challenges was developing a standardized and fast way to consume information across all of the supported systems such that data in a single report could be consumed from various sources. SAP achieved this through what they call the *Connection Concept* in the EPM Add-in.

In order to access a specific set of data contained in a cube, model, or data set within the EPM Add-in, a connection needs to be created to the source of data.

Connections are created and managed in the Connection Manager (see Figure 1.2).

Figure 1.2: Connection Manager

1.2.1 Different types of connections

The EPM Add-in is a very powerful tool that was designed to retrieve and input data from different EPM solutions at the same time. Data retrieval and input is dependent on the type of connection that is being established to a specific data source.

These data sources have been classified by SAP into the following categories.

Data Retrieval

▶ Microsoft SSAS cubes, including SSAS cubes created with SAP BusinessObjects Financial Consolidation, and cube designer.

▶ SAP NetWeaver BW InfoCubes, including BW InfoCubes created with SAP BusinessObjects Financial Consolidation, and cube designer.

▶ SAP BusinessObjects Profitability and Cost Management models.

▶ SAP BusinessObjects Strategy Management models.

▶ SAP BusinessObjects Planning and Consolidation, version for SAP NetWeaver, models - version 10.0 and version 10.1.

▶ SAP BusinessObjects Planning and Consolidation, version for the Microsoft platform, models.

▶ SAP HANA analytic views and EPM models.

Data Input

▶ SAP HANA EPM models.

▶ SAP NetWeaver BW Real-Time InfoCubes.

▶ SAP BusinessObjects Planning and Consolidation, version for SAP NetWeaver, models - version 10.0 and version 10.1.

▶ SAP BusinessObjects Planning and Consolidation, version for the Microsoft platform, models.

It's also important to note that the EPM Add-in replaces another SAP tool called Extended Analytics Analyzer 7.5 to retrieve data from the following data sources:

▶ SSAS cubes created with SAP BusinessObjects Financial Consolidation, cube designer.

▶ SAP NetWeaver BW InfoCubes created with SAP BusinessObjects Financial Consolidation, cube designer.

▶ SAP BusinessObjects Planning and Consolidation 7.5, version for SAP NetWeaver, models.

▶ SAP BusinessObjects Planning and Consolidation 7.5, version for the Microsoft platform, models.

Retrieving and inputting data can be done in the EPM Add-in depending on the different connection types that can be configured through the Connection Manager (see Figure 1.3).

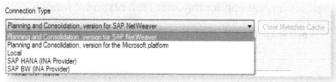

Figure 1.3: Connection types

Connection types can be classified as:

▶ Application Connections (INA, BPC, etc.).

▶ Local Connections.

Application connections are stored in different ways based on the type of application you are connecting to, whereas the local connections are stored on the desktop as .oqy files.

▶ There is a connections .xml file stored on the desktop that is created behind the scenes that the EPM Add-In reads from when launched. This .xml file stores the application connections created from the client.

Use case for the Connections.xml file

 The xml file is often used by IT departments within organizations to push pre-configured connections to end users so that they don't have to go through the steps of creating connections. Basically, if the connections file is pushed out to end users, then they have everything set up out of the box after installing the EPM Add-in.

The Connections.xml file is located by default under the following path on the desktop: C:\Users\%username%\AppData\Local\EPMOfficeClient

1.2.2 Creating a connection

Setting up a connection in the EPM Add-in is fairly easy and can be done by anyone. There's no need to have specialized technical knowledge to configure or maintain connections.

The steps to create a connection are outlined below.

1. Click on the Log On button from the EPM Add-in Ribbon (see Figure 1.4).

2. Select the connection type (see Figure 1.5).

3. Enter the server URL (see Figure 1.6).

4. Click on the CONNECT button and then enter your username and password (see Figure 1.7)

5. Select your environment and model and click on the GENERATE A CONNECTION NAME button or enter one manually (see Figure 1.8).

Finally, click on the OK button to finish setting up the connection.

Figure 1.4: Log on button in the EPM Ribbon

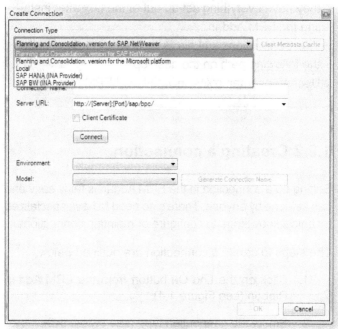

Figure 1.5: Select connection type

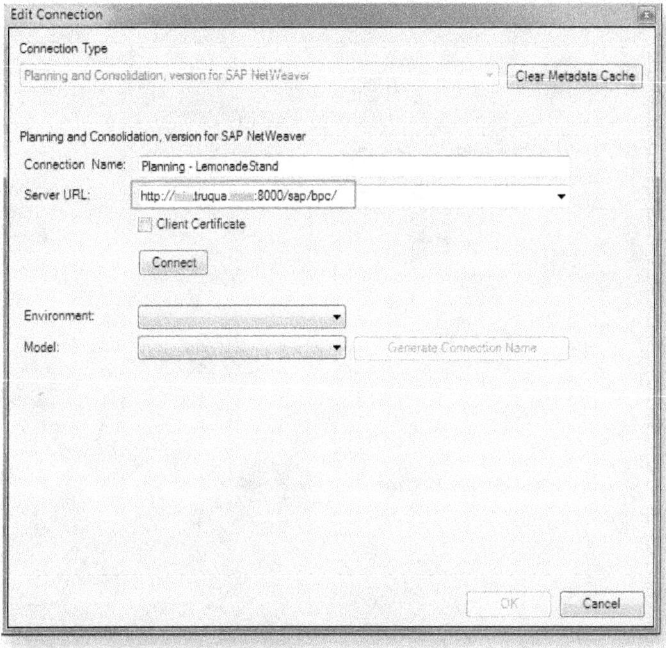

Figure 1.6: Enter server URL

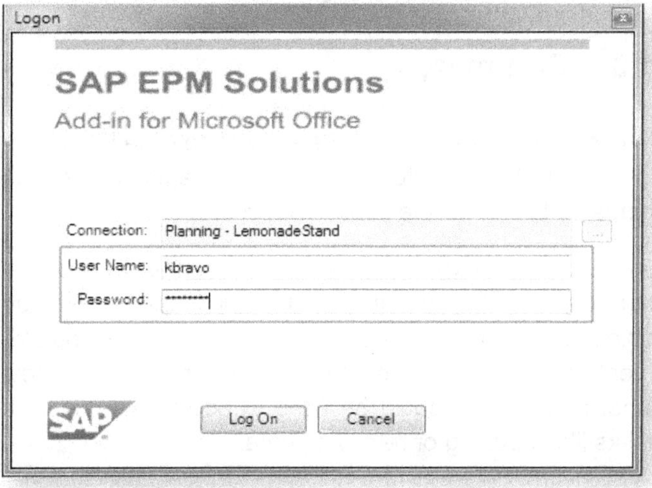

Figure 1.7: Enter credentials

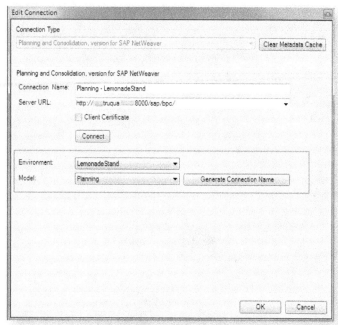

Figure 1.8: Generate connection

1.3 Summary

In this chapter, we covered the story of how the EPM Add-in came to fruition after a series of strategic acquisitions made by SAP over the past seven years.

In addition, we explored the concept and the steps to generate an EPM Connection. At this point, users should be able to generate new connections and understand the elements involved in the process. Users should now know what connections could be used to accomplish different tasks like inputting or retrieving data.

2. Case Study

To facilitate your understanding we will be working with a powerful learning tool: a sample business case. This chapter explains the details of the company and how they want to use the EPM Add-in. This case study will be referenced throughout the book to illustrate real business needs and how to meet them utilizing the EPM Add-in.

2.1 Case study overview

It is January 3, 2017. Rosie's Lemonade Company has been in business for almost six years now and is headquartered in Chicago, IL. The company has a strong presence in North America (Canada, United States, and Mexico) with over 500 distribution routes and several clients that range from local lemonade stands to big retail shops.

Figure 2.1: Rosie's Lemonade Company

Rosie's Lemonade Company has a wide portfolio of products that target several market segments, which has grown rapidly over the years due to its excellent management and the successful operations of its business.

In the most recent board meeting, Rosie and other executives discussed the importance of keeping their financial planning processes in a centrally managed information system. They are now operating in three different countries and the ability to access critical financial information is a must.

As the CFO, Rosie knows that most of their planning processes are being done in Excel and it's hard to keep track of the different versions of their planning documents and keep everyone updated with the right information, especially when they need to make critical decisions.

Some of her analysts struggle to fulfill Rosie's expectations when preparing the financial reports for Rosie's meetings with the Executive Committee, mostly because each one has different templates and everyone owns a unique version of truth.

In a recent survey, some key managers at the company expressed their interest in using a tool to generate their monthly forecasts, enable them to make comparisons against actuals, load their transactional data from their SAP Business Warehouse, and improve their financial forecasting process by making it more dynamic. One big constraint to adopting the tool is management's fear that their analysts will struggle to learn how to make the same types of analysis they are currently performing in the new tool. In addition, they fear that the tool will not be adopted because there's a strong resistance to change within the organization.

2.2   Case study details

Rosie's Lemonade Company has been using SAP ERP (ECC) to keep track of their business transactions and most of the analytics are run using SAP NetWeaver BW for decision-making. However, their analysts are constantly complaining that they spend a lot of time exporting the data from BW into Excel to perform their calculations (allocations, distributions, etc.) and to build or manage their budget and forecast.

Management recognizes that a streamlined planning process will help the company overcome their growth challenges.

Since the company already works with Excel spreadsheets, management decided to leverage that familiarity with Excel to avoid low adoption rates.

After a core meeting, Rosie's Lemonade Company made the strategic decision to implement SAP Business Planning and Consolidations 10.1 version for NetWeaver and leverage the EPM Add-in (an Excel Add-in) as a unified tool for entering budgets, monitoring the forecasting process, and to keep track of different versions instead of having to deal with several files on user desktops.

One of the desirable features that the board is very happy with is the ability to leverage their existing BW platform. By leveraging the existing SAP BW they can tap into the important investments they have been making over the years to build a solid solution.

The key factors that led Rosie's Lemonade Company to use the EPM Add-in as their unified tool for their financial processes were the following:

▶ The tool will reduce their planning cycles and enable multiple iterations of analysis without having to deal with several versions of the same files.

▶ A reduction in change management costs, as resistance to change will be less since their analysts are already working with Excel.

▶ The tool is easy to adopt and learn since it's based on Excel, a tool the business is already working with.

▶ The tool will leverage the existing investment made in SAP BW to pull in sales and costs in order to build executive dashboards through the EPM Add-in saving costs and capitalizing on the money and effort already invested.

▶ Flexibility to unify different data sources into one common report.

▶ Security features enabling multiple groups to work simultaneously with their individual sets of sensitive data like headcounts, capital expenditure projects, and sales projections without permitting cross group access to the data.

At this point there should be a sound understanding of Rosie's Lemonade Company's requirements and why there is a strong desire to develop a streamlined financial process by leveraging the EPM Add-in's powerful features.

2.3   Summary

In this chapter, we explored a business case scenario that will be used throughout the book to explain key concepts that users should know when working with the EPM Add-in. Understanding these key concepts will facilitate the learning process and guide the reader through each chapter following one thread connecting each key concept to the next.

Rosie's Lemonade Company's business case leverages several years of industry knowledge used to put together a case that is accurate and close to reality. It depicts real life scenarios and accurate client requirements that occur during a project implementation.

3. EPM Add-in reports and input schedules

When using the EPM Add-in the use of native functions and features is available in Excel such as standard formulas and VBA, while simultaneously augmenting them with additional functionality such as sending and retrieving data from the database. In simple words, it's Excel with extended functionality.

> **What do most companies use today to track their financials at a management level?**
>
> Excel is used across industries and it's by far one of the most popular tools to keep track of financials at a management level. One of the challenges that most companies face is to successfully manage several Excel files and versions that may contain different versions of the truth. The EPM Add-in, in conjunction with the SAP EPM Suite, addresses this problem by centrally managing the "Excel Hell" which reduces its complexity (see Figure 3.1).

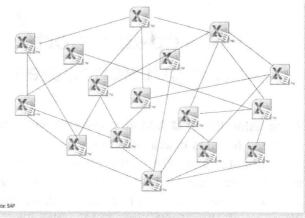

Source: SAP

Figure 3.1: The complexity of "Excel Hell"

The EPM Add-in is a client side component with expansive functionality that includes: offline analysis, advanced EPM functions, multi-source reporting, book publishing, planning and consolidation features, etc. In every implementation this front-end interface will deliver a standardized way to perform basically two operations. First, retrieving data from a source system (i.e. SAP BW or SAP HANA) and second, sending data back which keeps a database up to date with the latest information.

EPM Add-in Version and Service Pack

In this book, we are working with the SAP EPM Add-in Service Pack 18 used with BPC 10.1. SAP regularly releases patches and service packs, but all the functionality demonstrated in this book should remain relevant in the future.

3.1   Report building basics

Rosie's Lemonade Company will use the SAP EPM Add-in for Excel as the main interface to create reports and templates for analysts across business units and in day-to-day running of the business.

The add-in provides several tools to facilitate analysis by enabling the users to slice and dice information in a very similar (albeit, more powerful) way to the pivot table functionality in Excel.

It's important that Rosie and her implementation team always keep in mind the following overall layout rules so that the EPM Add-in can correctly render each report they build (see Figure 3.2).

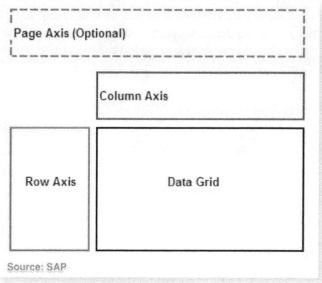

Figure 3.2: Overall layout rules

This layout structure needs to be followed every time to ensure that your reports will work and also, to make your reports easier to understand for others.

Mandatory items on every report are the column and the row axes. These two will auto generate the data grid once the EPM Add-in retrieves data from the database.

The only requirement when defining the position of these two axes is that the columns should always appear at least one row above the row axis, while the latter can appear to the right or to the left of the column axes at any time.

The page axis acts as a filter and it's an optional para-meter. It can appear anywhere as long as it's above the column axis.

Each dimension or hierarchy can only appear once in the whole layout, this means that you cannot place one di-mension in two different column cells (see Figure 3.3).

Figure 3.3: Dimension layout restrictions

Key business planning and consolidation concepts

 In this section, we will describe some key business planning and consolidation concepts (BPC, as of 10.x release) that we will reference in the book to ensure that you have a better understanding of the content in each chapter.

An Environment is the starting point of the modeling process for SAP Business Planning and Consolidation implementations. Its purpose is to include the models associated with business segments created to meet client requirements, such as headcount planning, legal or management consolidations, cost of goods sold planning, etc.

The base environment delivered by SAP out-of-the-box is called "EnvironmentShell".

A **Model** is a collection of dimensions built inside of an environment. These are designed to meet the planning and consolidation requirements of an organization.

Dimensions, also known as characteristics in the BW space, are considered the cornerstone of the Business Planning and Consolidation architecture. They hold dimension members with the purpose of describing elements of a business (i.e. accounts, legal entities, plants, sales channels, etc.) Each dimension can house several **hierarchies**, which are logical relationships with other members in the same dimension.

A **dimension member** represents a single value within a dimension. The structure of a dimension member is made up of an alphanumerical ID, a description, properties and a key to denote its placement in the dimension hierarchy. To put all of this in simple words, we can think of dimension members as an individual that integrates a family (dimension), which has ranks (a hierarchical structure). Each member has its own properties (for example; occupation, age, hobbies, etc.)

3.2 Standard templates – What comes out of the box?

SAP delivers a set of templates that help clients like Rosie's Lemonade Company modify and create new reports by using the templates as both building blocks and examples of what they can accomplish with the add-in right out of the box (see Figure 3.4).

To access these templates you need to click on the OPEN button in the EPM Ribbon and then the OPEN SERVER REPORT FOLDER (see Figure 3.5).

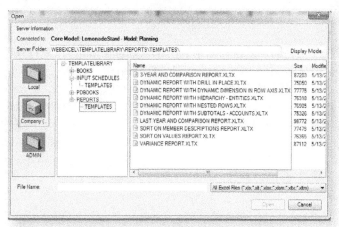

Figure 3.4: Pre-delivered SAP report templates

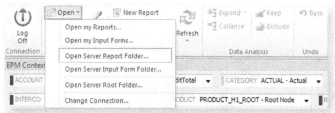

Figure 3.5: Open server report folder

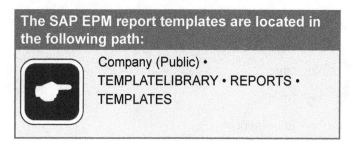

The SAP EPM report templates are located in the following path:

Company (Public) •
TEMPLATELIBRARY • REPORTS •
TEMPLATES

3.3   Building a report from scratch

Before jumping into the world of report building we will take a brief guided tour of the EPM Ribbon, the EPM Context, and the EPM Pane. This information will familiarize you with basic terminology that we will cover and explore in the next several chapters of this book.

3.3.1 EPM Ribbon

This is the main interface end users leverage to interact with the EPM Add-in. The EPM Ribbon contains links to all of the functionality that the tool offers and follows Microsoft's standard layout, formatting, and iconography. This standardized design philosophy makes adoption easier among users already familiar with MS Office (see Figure 3.6).

Figure 3.6: EPM Ribbon

The following list contains the key EPM Ribbon buttons:

► Log On/Off

► Open

► Save

► Edit Report

► New Report

► Refresh

► Save Data

► Options

► More

With these EPM buttons end users will be able to:

► Log on and off to any connection available in the Connection Manager (see Figure 1.2).

► Open and save reports to and from an application server.

► Create new EPM Reports and edit their current definitions with the EDIT REPORT button.

► Pull the latest data of an EPM report by using the REFRESH button.

► Send data to the database using with the SAVE DATA button.

► Set additional options to control the behavior of a report.

► Access the EPM Logging framework from the MORE button, etc.

3.3.2 EPM Context

The EPM Context provides a view into the data being reported or planned against providing a way to quickly modify the data intersection allowing for easy access to all authorized data within a given model (see Figure 3.7).

EPM member selector default behavior

 It's important to note that every dimension that hasn't been explicitly assigned to any of the axes (column, row, or page axes) will be driven by the selections displayed in the EPM Context.

The members that are displayed in each dimension from the EPM Context are authorization sensitive, you will only be able to visualize the members that you have been granted access to display and/or input against (see Figure 3.7).

Figure 3.7: EPM Context

The EPM Context saves the history of the recently used members. The recent history is accessible in the drop down menu that appears when the black arrows on each dimension selection box are clicked.

If the user selects the SELECT OTHER MEMBERS option in the dropdown menu, the member selector pop-up box appears giving the end user access to all authorized member values (see Figure 3.8).

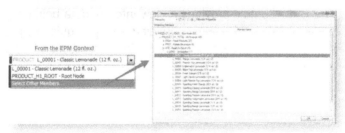

Figure 3.8: Member selector

From the member selector window, the way in which the dimension members are displayed can be changed.

There are three display options that you can choose at any time (see Figure 3.9).

▶ ID

▶ Description

▶ ID – Description

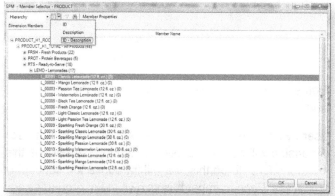

Figure 3.9: Member display options

In addition to using the member selector, it is possible to change the member display in a report from the Report Editor by using the DISPLAY OPTIONS button (see Figure 3.9) from there. We will be using these options frequently when we start building Rosie's first report. The way users display members can be changed at any time and will not affect the functionality of the report itself.

The add-in has search and filtering capabilities that users can use to enhance the way they build reports. To access the search functionality users can click on the binoculars in the EPM Member Selector window, or by using the shortcut (Ctrl + F) (see Figure 3.10).

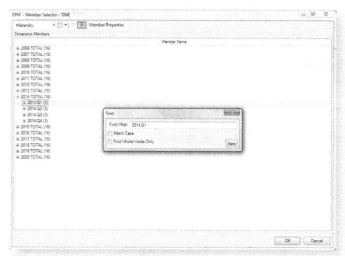

Figure 3.10: Finding members in the EPM member selector

Users with a broader knowledge of the structure of each dimension will be able to use the filtering capabilities that the tool offers. To do this, we will introduce the concept of properties. Each member has its own set of properties and depending on the dimension type, there are certain required and pre-delivered properties such as account type, currency, or entity. The EPM Add-in also supports reading custom properties.

There are various ways to display member properties:

▶ From the EPM Member Selector (see Figure 3.11).

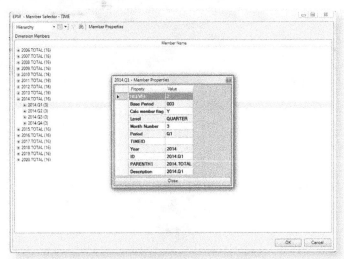

Figure 3.11: Member properties

▶ By using the properties option when you right click a member directly in a report (EPM • PROPERTIES) (see Figure 3.12).

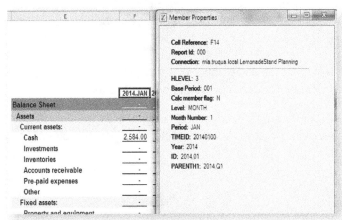

Figure 3.12: Right click a member in an EPM Report

▶ From the EPM Ribbon under the More button •
PROPERTIES. Note that you have to place your
cursor in an active EPM Member cell within a report for this option to work (see Figure 3.13).

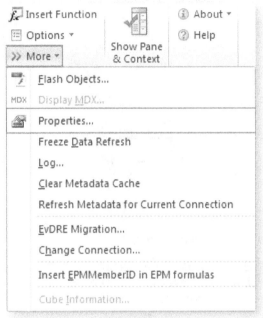

*Figure 3.13: Displaying a member's properties from the
EPM Ribbon*

Now that we know how to display properties for a specific
member, we can explore the concept further.

Properties help to describe a dimension member by ex-
tending the amount of characteristics that are directly associated with it.

Extending the properties concept

 If we define a dimension named employee we could define properties to extend the set of available information for a given member providing additional detail such as an employee's social security number, selected health plan, employee type, etc.

The use of properties in reporting enables the grouping of members, filtering members with ease, and the ability to quickly distinguish between nodes and base members.

In the EPM Selector window there's a filter icon that users can click to access the filtering options that are available via the EPM Add-in. This is a very powerful utility that can help users build more advanced reports (see Figure 3.14).

Figure 3.14: Setting up filters based on a member's property

3.3.3 EPM Pane

Before jumping in to the report building exercise, there is another part of the EPM Add-in that all users should know and be familiar with, the EPM Pane. This is one of the most important elements of the EPM Add-in.

With this pane users will be able to change how their reports look on the fly with very little effort.

The EPM pane is composed of three main sections. Each section is aligned to the report structure mentioned earlier in this chapter (see section 3.3) complemented by additional options listed below (see Figure 3.15). They include:

▶ Data Connections

▶ Dimension list

▶ Page Axis

▶ Row Axis

▶ Column Axis

▶ Defer Layout Update function

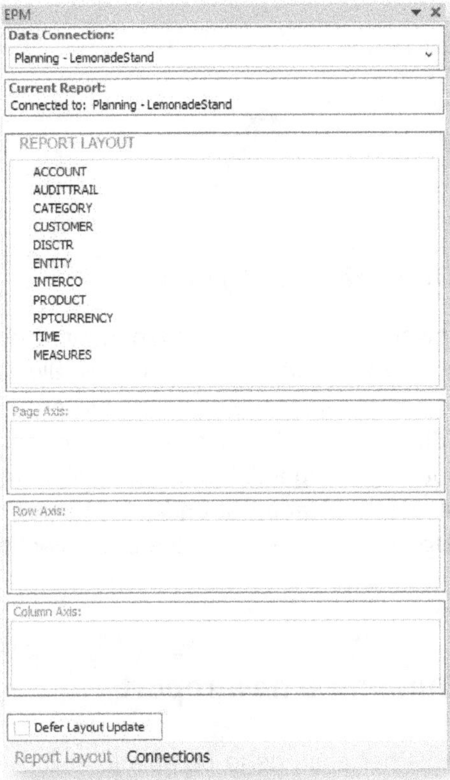

Figure 3.15: EPM Pane

The EPM Add-in allows users to place different reports in a single Excel sheet. These reports can be associated with the same connection, but the add-in goes beyond that by allowing multi-source reporting which enables users to connect to multiple information sources across models, cubes, and queries simultaneously.

From the EPM pane users will be able to display the connections of the report in which they are working, see where this report is defined within the Excel sheet, and more (see Figure 3.16).

Figure 3.16: Current report definition

A very powerful feature that's often ignored by users is the **Defer Layout Update** function. This allows a report builder to select dimensions, switch the order in which they are displayed, and select members for each dimension without triggering a database pull. When making several changes to a report at once, the use of the **Defer Layout Update** function can save a substantial amount of time.

3.3.4 Building a new report

Rosie wants her analysts to be able to build a basic balance sheet. She wants to be able to see different views of her data easily, as well as understand the different types of analysis that the EPM Add-in will facilitate.

To do so, she and her analysts will follow these steps to build a basic report.

The first thing is to click on the NEW REPORT button in the EPM Ribbon.

After clicking this button the EPM Report Editor will appear in a separate window.

The EPM Report Editor is the main place where a report can be defined. Users must select which dimensions will appear on the axes and what members they want to display.

Users can define a report by dragging and dropping the dimensions into the specific regions defined in of the Report Editor.

Within the EPM Add-in when a dimension member is selected, a behavior is applied to how the data is displayed. Whether a member is displayed by itself, with its children, or in another manner is what's called the relationship concept.

Default member selection

 The report editor defaults each dimension to the members selected in the Context Bar. The default relationship is 'Member and Children' which means not only the selected member will be displayed, but that member's direct children as well. To hardcode a member, users have to change the defaulted selection to the desired dimension members. Otherwise, each user will get different members depending on their context selections.

The relationship concept is critical for users to be able to display the right members on each report. This concept is how relationships are defined in the member selector.

When a relationship is selected, the report will automatically be updated with members that correspond to the relationship (see Figure 3.17).

- ► Member Only

- ► Member and Children

- ► Children

- ► Member and Descendants

- ► Descendants

- ► Base Level

- ► Same Level

- ► Siblings

- ► Member and Ascendants

- ► Ascendants

- ► Member and Base Level

- ► Member Offset

- ► Member Property

- ► Blank Member

- ► All Members

- ► Dimension Property

Some members have a special behavior

 Blank members, all members and dimension property options will only appear if no member is selected in the EPM Member Selector.

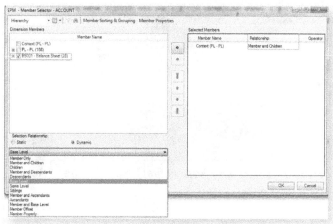

Figure 3.17: Defining member relationships

Building Rosie's first balance sheet

To build a balance sheet, Rosie needs to make sure that she has at least one dimension selected on the column axis and the row axis. Rosie will then drag the account dimension to the rows and time dimension to the columns. She will select the relationship member and descendants for the account dimension, and member and base level for the time dimension. Once complete, she just needs to click the OK button and she will be done building her first basic balance sheet (Figure 3.18 and Figure 3.19).

After hitting OK in the Report Editor, her report should look like Figure 3.20.

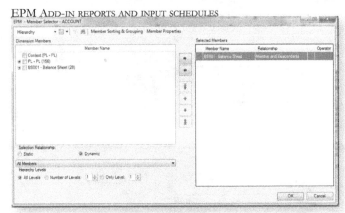

Figure 3.18: Building Rosie's first balance sheet – Account dimension

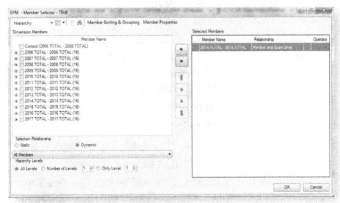

Figure 3.19: Building Rosie's first balance sheet – Time dimension

	2012.TOTAL	2013.TOTAL	2014.TOTAL
Balance Sheet	0.00	0.00	0.00
Assets	99769.38	107750.93	116371.00
Current assets:	38569.96	41655.56	44988.00
Cash	8414.78	9087.96	9815.00
Investments	0.00	0.00	0.00
Inventories	665.29	718.52	776.00
Accounts receivable	4603.05	4971.30	5369.00
Pre-paid expenses	0.00	0.00	0.00
Other	24886.83	26877.78	29028.00
Fixed assets:	6667.52	7200.93	7777.00
Property and equipment	10089.16	10896.30	11768.00
Leasehold improvements	0.00	0.00	0.00
Equity and other investments	0.00	0.00	0.00
Less accumulated depreciation	-3421.64	-3695.37	-3991.00
Other assets:	54531.89	58894.44	63606.00
Goodwill	54531.89	58894.44	63606.00
Liabilities and owner's equity	99769.38	107750.93	116371.00
Current liabilities:	23979.77	25898.15	27970.00
Accounts payable	12544.58	13548.15	14632.00
Accrued wages	7927.81	8562.04	9247.00
Accrued compensation	0.00	0.00	0.00
Income taxes payable	0.00	0.00	0.00
Unearned revenue	0.00	0.00	0.00
Other	3507.37	3787.96	4091.00
Long-term liabilities:	10104.60	10912.96	11786.00
Mortgage payable	10104.60	10912.96	11786.00
Owner's equity:	65685.01	70939.81	76615.00
Investment capital	65685.01	70939.81	76615.00
Accumulated retained earnings	0.00	0.00	0.00

Figure 3.20: Rosie's first balance sheet

Versioning

It's important that Rosie and her analysts always save the reports being built to the server. Using different versions to keep track of the changes being made is a good practice when report building. It's also important to save a copy of a working report before making significant changes to it. This will save a report builder the headache of having to fix a report that broke after making adjustments. It is always a good idea to have a backup!

3.4   Formatting

Now that Rosie has built her first balance sheet, she wants to give it a corporate look and at the same time, she wants the EPM Add-in to remember her formatting selections every time she changes the report definition or the members displayed in the report

To do so, we will explore the dynamic formatting capabilities that the EPM Add-in provides.

The first step is to click on the VIEW FORMATS button available in the EPM Ribbon. The add-in will generate a new Excel sheet called **EPM Formatting Sheet** (see Figure 3.21). The sheet follows a four-tier structure comprised of the following components:

▶ Hierarchy Level Formatting

▶ Dimension Member/Property Formatting

▶ Row and Column Banding

▶ Page Axis Formatting

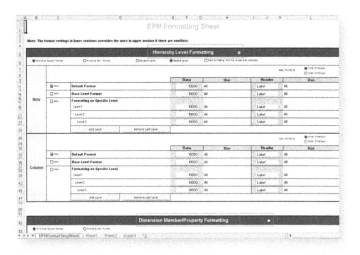

Figure 3.21: EPM formatting sheet

▶ Each one of these tiers control different aspects of the report and we will explore each one of them in detail below.

Tier Priority

 The format settings in lower tiers overrides the ones in upper tiers if there are conflicts.

▶ Each one of the tiers share almost the same structure and options where users can define formatting for the dimension's headers and/or intersection data.

▶ Tiers set the format according to the columns or rows and each one has a separate section in the EPM Formatting Sheet. Users have the option to switch the priority of the formatting from rows to columns and vice versa.

3.4.1 Hierarchy level formatting

This section controls the formatting that applies to rows and columns for all members and dimensions defined in the report definition.

3.4.2 Dimension member/Property formatting

This section controls the formatting for specific members, local members, members that share a specific property, input ready members, etc.

Key member definitions

 Local Members are defined within a report and do not belong to a specific dimension. These can be used to store calculations, or as placeholders to comply with formatting requirements.

An **Input ready member** is any member in a dimension that hasn't been defined as a parent or a calculated node within a hierarchy. They are also known as "base level members".

3.4.3 Row and column banding

This section enables users to define column and row banding to make reports that have multiple rows or columns easier to read.

3.4.4 Page axis formatting

This section controls the page axis formatting. This is the simplest of all the tiers since you can only format the area in which the page axis is rendered. This can be generic formatting for the entire axis or specific to a dimension in the page axis.

3.4.5 Sheet options

The EPM Ribbon has an OPTIONS button; which plays a very important role when users start to use dynamic formatting. When a user clicks on the OPTIONS button, the EPM Add-in will bring up the EPM – Sheets Options window.

This window has several options and menus and it affects all of the existing reports in a single Excel sheet.

The Sheet Options Menu is composed of the following elements:

▶ General

▶ Formatting

▶ Refresh

▶ Protection

General tab controls how to:

▶ Display members after performing an expansion (drill-down).

▶ Transform a report into an input schedule by checking the USE AS INPUT FORM checkbox.

▶ Activate member recognition and local member recognition.

▶ Select where to display the placement of totals.

▶ Suppress rows or columns where there are zeros or empty values.

▶ Change how to display comments.

Dimension member expansions

 You can trigger an expansion by double clicking on a parent member or, by selecting a parent member and clicking on the EXPAND button from the EPM Ribbon.

Formatting tab controls how to:

▶ Control the indentation used when displaying members.

▶ Manage how to display a dimension member.

▶ Enable the ability to auto fit column width.

▶ Turn on repetition on the column / row headers.

▶ Manage whether or not to display the dimension names.

▶ Set default values for empty cells in the report cells.

▶ Turn on the dynamic formatting functionality.

Refresh tab controls how to:

▶ Configure formulas to be kept in a report after refreshing it. This is applicable when users input formulas inside of the data grid.

▶ Show source data in the comments. Which is one of the most requested features since this option displays source values retrieved from the database as comments, even when a formula is inputted in that cell.

▶ Calculate parents in hierarchies (with an Excel formula) instead of performing calculations in the backend. Especially useful when inputting data since this option will generate an Excel formula that allows real-time simulations.

▶ Manage the refresh behavior when opening, expanding members, or saving a report to the server.

▶ Show unauthorized cell text, which allows users to test security settings by displaying when a user is not authorized to display specific members.

▶ Force the original report definition in a report, avoiding changes to the report editor member selector when performing expand or collapse operations.

▶ Keep formulas static, which means that a formula will always reference the same cell even if it's being moved around the report.

Protection tab controls how to:

▶ Protect a worksheet or workbook against changes.

▶ Set up a password to lock or unlock a worksheet or workbook.

▶ Enable users to perform specific tasks on a report.

In the following section, we will focus on the formatting tab so that Rosie can enable formatting by selecting the APPLY DYNAMIC FORMATTING checkbox enabling the configuration within the EPM Formatting Sheet.

In addition to formatting, Rosie will be able to control indentation, the repetition of member headers for columns and rows, the default value for empty cells, and more (see Figure 3.22).

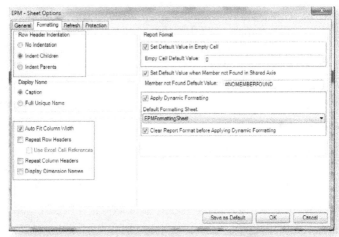

Figure 3.22: EPM – Sheet options in the formatting tab

3.5   Step by step: Building a formatted report

Now let's help Rosie format her balance sheet. As mentioned previously, she needs to click on the VIEW FORMATS button in the EPM Ribbon to trigger the automatic generation of the EPM Formatting Sheet.

By tweaking some of the parameters in the hierarchy level formatting section of the EPM Formatting Sheet, we are able to create a very simple dynamic format that looks good and serves Rosie's need to give a corporate look to her balance sheet.

These very basic modifications to the EPM Formatting Sheet can be observed in Figure 3.23.

Rosie configured a level based color schema using standard formatting from the Home Tab within the Excel Ribbon.

She also changed the format of the cells containing data to a number format with two decimal places.

Rosie also defined a default label format bolding and centering the column headers, while the rows should remain left justified.

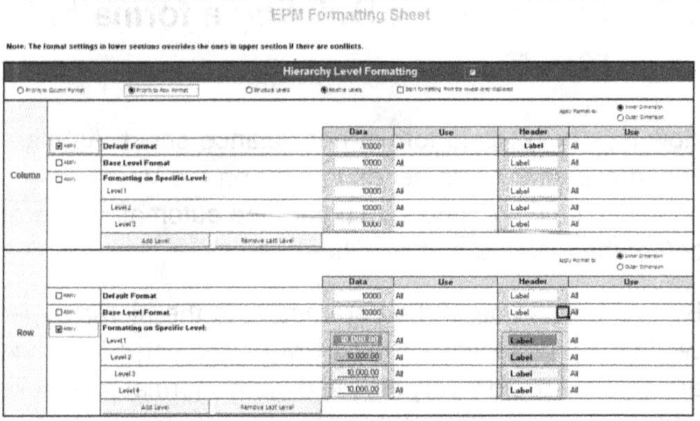

Figure 3.23: Setting up Rosie's EPM formatting sheet

Rosie inserted Rosie's Lemonade Company logo as a picture without any trouble since this is Excel functionality and she already knew how to perform this activity without guidance.

By clicking the REFRESH button from the EPM Ribbon, her balance sheet is now in alignment with the corporate rules that Rosie's Lemonade Company mandates according to their branding and formatting guidelines.

This was a surprise to Rosie as she found that formatting is very simple and end users can play around with all of the settings that are available in the EPM Formatting Sheet. She also realized that this exercise could be executed multiple times with minimal risk of end users breaking the report.

She was given the advice to keep dynamic formatting simple since this activity is performed by the add-in on each desktop and underpowered workstations could be affected if done wrong.

Over using formatting features

 Report designers and end users have to keep in mind that formatting is executed every single time a report is refreshed, so it's important to keep it simple to avoid performance issues.

Rosie was very happy with the results and she realized that with just some small tweaks to the EPM Formatting Sheet (see Figure 3.24), her balance sheet looked more professional. She could also change the layout on the fly without an implementation team, or IT department support.

Rosie's Lemonade

	2014.TOTAL Actual	2015.TOTAL Actual	2016.TOTAL Actual	2017.TOTAL Actual
Balance Sheet				
Assets	116,371.00	118,844.74	121,372.34	123,955.02
Current assets:	44,988.00	45,949.21	46,947.47	47,993.74
Cash	9,815.00	10,011.30	10,211.53	10,415.76
Investments	-	-	-	-
Inventories	776.00	799.28	839.24	906.38
Accounts receivable	5,369.00	5,530.07	5,695.97	5,866.85
Pre-paid expenses	-	-	-	-
Other	29,028.00	29,608.56	30,200.73	30,804.75
Fixed assets:	7,777.00	8,017.41	8,249.19	8,462.09
Property and equipment	11,768.00	12,003.36	12,243.43	12,488.30
Leasehold improvements	-	-	-	-
Equity and other investments	-	-	-	-
Less accumulated depreciation	(3,991.00)	(3,985.95)	(3,994.24)	(4,026.21)
Other assets:	63,606.00	64,878.12	66,175.68	67,499.20
Goodwill	63,606.00	64,878.12	66,175.68	67,499.20
Liabilities and owner's equity	116,371.00	118,844.74	121,372.34	123,955.02
Current liabilities:	27,970.00	28,675.72	29,399.94	30,143.17
Accounts payable	14,632.00	15,070.96	15,523.09	15,988.78
Accrued wages	9,247.00	9,431.94	9,620.58	9,812.99
Accrued compensation	-	-	-	-
Income taxes payable	-	-	-	-
Unearned revenue	-	-	-	-
Other	4,091.00	4,172.82	4,256.28	4,341.40
Long-term liabilities:	11,786.00	12,021.72	12,262.15	12,507.40
Mortgage payable	11,786.00	12,021.72	12,262.15	12,507.40
Owner's equity:	76,615.00	78,147.30	79,710.25	81,304.45
Investment capital	76,615.00	78,147.30	79,710.25	81,304.45
Accumulated retained earnings	-	-	-	-

Figure 3.24: Rosie's formatted balance sheet

65

3.6   Building an input schedule

Building an input schedule with the EPM Add-in is incredibly simple. Report designers and users follow the same steps to build a report; there is one minor difference, a checkbox.

From the EPM Ribbon choose the SHEET OPTIONS button and click on the USE AS INPUT FORM checkbox (see Figure 3.25).

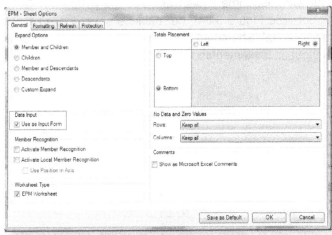

Figure 3.25: Converting a report to an input schedule

After you enable this checkbox users will now be able to input data into the business planning and consolidation models or Input-ready Queries by clicking the SAVE DATA button in the EPM Ribbon.

3.7　Using EPM save functions

The EPM Add-in has three functions that allow users to save data to the server from a report without making it input ready. This can be enabled by identifying specific cells to attach one of the following functions:

► EPMSaveData

► EPMSaveDataOnly

► EPMSaveComment

3.7.1 EPMSaveData

This function enables you embed the ability to send and retrieve transactional data from the database within a cell. The function formula requires that the intersection of data be fully qualified. This means that every dimension in the model requires a member to be specified within the formula. If a member is not specified in the formula, the selected values within the EPM context will be defaulted. It is important to remember that if the intent is to write enable a cell, the members selected need to be base level members.

When configuring the formula, dimension members can be specified explicitly or referenced from a cell. After entering the formula, the report needs to be refreshed in order for it to become write enabled.

To trigger the send function users have to click on the SAVE DATA button in the EPM Ribbon (see Figure 3.26).

The structure of the function is the following:

▶ Cell

▶ Connection Name (Optional)

▶ Member from 1 to X (X being the number of dimensions available in your model or query)

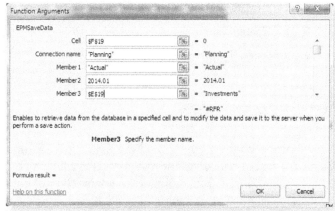

Figure 3.26: EPMSaveData from the Formula Editor

3.7.2 EPMSaveDataOnly

This function enables to embed within a cell the ability to send transactional data to the database. If a member is not specified in the formula it will be defaulted from the EPM context.

Users can either hardcode dimension members, or reference them from a cell. After entering the formula users have to refresh the report before the cell will become write enabled. Remember, in order to write data to the database, the members selected need to be leaf nodes, members that exist at the base level of a dimension hierarchy.

To trigger the send function users have to click on the SAVE DATA button in the EPM Ribbon (see Figure 3.27).

The structure of the function is the following:

▶ Cell

▶ Connection Name (Optional)

▶ Member from 1 to X (X being the number of dimensions available in your model or query)

EPMSaveData vs. EPMSaveDataOnly

 The main difference between EPMSaveData and EPMSaveDataOnly is that the latter won't retrieve data; it will only send it to the server.

Figure 3.27: EPMSaveDataOnly from the Formula Editor

3.7.3 EPMSaveComment

This function enables you to save comments, or modify existing comments. This is especially useful if you are building financial statements and users need to input comments to make specific notes for regulatory or management requirements.

If a member is not specified in the formula, it will be taken from the context.

Users can either hardcode dimension members, or reference them from a cell. After entering the formula users will need to refresh the report before the ability to save or update comments is enabled.

To trigger the send function users have to click on the SAVE DATA button in the EPM Ribbon (see Figure 3.28).

The structure of the function is as follows:

- ▶ Cell

- ▶ Connection Name (Optional)

- ▶ Member from 1 to X (X being the number of dimensions available in your model or query)

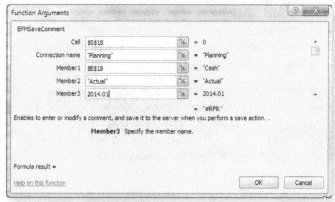

Figure 3.28: EPMSaveComment from the Formula Editor

3.8 Using Built In Planning Functions

The EPM Add-in has a set of built in planning features to facilitate entering data into an input schedule.

These planning functions can be executed from the EPM Ribbon; users can find them under the drop down menu 'SPREAD, TREND...'. There are three planning functions (see Figure 3.29):

► Spread

► Trend

► Weight

Figure 3.29: Spread, trend and weight Functions

3.8.1 Spread

The spread feature enables you to take a value and allocate it across the selected destination cells.

Using the spread function

This can be used to do a "peanut butter spread" of an expense across multiple months in an input schedule.

3.8.2 Trend

The trend feature takes a value or percentage and grows it by a factor among selected cells. This option places the source value in the first cell of the destination range. Each subsequent cell in the destination increases by the amount or percentage specified.

Using the trend function

This function is especially useful when you are forecasting the following period. Financial planners like it because it makes it easier to calculate trends without the need to perform backend calculations.

3.8.3 Weight

The weight feature lets you allocate a set of values by weighted factors in your spreadsheet.

Using the weight function

 A use case for this function is to perform data disaggregation in a spreadsheet with pre-defined allocation percentages or wages.

3.8.4 Incorporating spread, trend, and weight

The beauty of these planning functions is that they are always available to end users from the EPM Ribbon. It doesn't require additional configuration and can be used by end users with minimal training or guidance.

Some users like to assign these functions to a series of VBA buttons to avoid going through the dropdown menu and switching tabs every time. This can be achieved by leveraging the FPMXLClient library and its functions.

We will discuss this use case further in section 5.1.

How to create VBA buttons

 When building an Excel model some-times it can help to "jazz up" the end-user experience by embedding some addition-al user controls like buttons or drop down menus.

In order to extend Excel through Visual Basic for Applications (VBA), a user needs to enable the developer tab, which is not shown by default. The steps to enable the developer ribbon differ depending on the Microsoft Excel version being used.

In Excel 2010 users have to click on FILE • SELECT OP-TIONS • CUSTOMIZE RIBBON MENU and check the selection box to the left of the developer option from the main tabs drop box.

To add a VBA button, users need to go to the devel-oper tab, click the INSERT button and select the button from the FORM CONTROL section.

3.9 Steps by step – Building an input schedule

Rosie would like to project Rosie's Lemonade Company's balance sheet data for 2018.

By doing a linear regression of their sales information from previous years, Rosie's Lemonade Sales Director estimates 5% flat growth in sales leading to a direct increase in their accounts receivables, accounts payables, and inventories.

Rosie wants to be able to generate an input form based on the balance sheet she already built without making major

changes. One of her requirements is that the input schedule can be used in an iterative process where multiple
revisions are created. Rosie wants to be able to evaluate
and change the results of her predictions in real time.

The first thing that she will do is open her existing report
from the EPM Ribbon • Open Server Root Folder Button
• Reports • Select Rosie's Lemonade Balance Sheet (see
Figure 3.30).

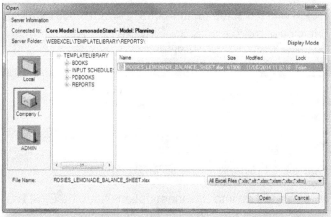

Figure 3.30: Converting a report into an input schedule

Then, Rosie will add the category dimension to the column axis as depicted in Figure 3.31 and select ACTUAL
member for previous years data and the forecast version,
FCST_11_1 for all 2018 data. Since the balance sheet is a
snapshot in time of what a company owns and owes, she
wants to input her predictions in the last month of 2018.

Modifying the EPMOlapMemberO formula

Setting up the right members in the category dimension for each month is critical. Rosie's Lemonade loads actuals on a monthly basis and Rosie needs to keep track of her forecasted versions to measure the accuracy of her predictions. She needs to use different members to avoid overwriting her forecasted data with the actual values coming in from each month. It is possible to modify the EPMOlapMemberO formula to achieve this as depicted in Figure 3.31.

Figure 3.31: Changing the EPMOlapMemberO formula

Now she will go into the sheet options from the EPM Ribbon to convert the report to an input schedule from the General Tab (Figure 3.32).

Figure 3.32: Converting a report to an input schedule

Rosie is expecting a 5% increase from 2017 to 2018, which she will reflect as a formula. In order to maintain this formula, she will need to check the KEEP FORMULA ON DATA option from the Refresh Tab within the Sheet Options (see Figure 3.33).

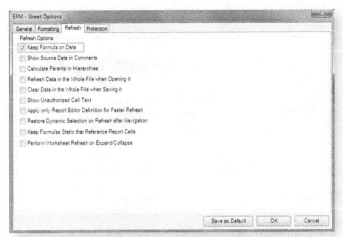

Figure 3.33: Keeping Excel formulas after refreshing a report

The next step is to hit the REFRESH button for the active balance sheet report and then make sure that each member in the page, column, and row axes is a base member.

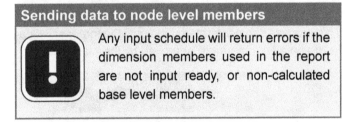

Sending data to node level members

Any input schedule will return errors if the dimension members used in the report are not input ready, or non-calculated base level members.

After this, she can input a simple Excel formula referencing the cells where Rosie's Lemonade Company input schedule is displaying the accounts relevant for accounts receivables, accounts payable, and inventories (see Figure 3.34).

Rosie's Lemonade

	2014.DEC Actual	2015.DEC Actual	2016.DEC Actual	2017.DEC Actual	2018.DEC FCST 1+11
Balance Sheet					
Assets	116,371.00	118,844.74	121,372.34	123,955.02	126,434.12
Current assets:	44,988.00	45,949.21	46,947.47	47,993.74	49,156.81
Cash	9,815.00	10,011.30	10,211.53	10,415.76	10,624.07
Investments	-	-	-	-	-
Inventories	776.00	799.28	839.24	906.38	951.70
Accounts receivable	5,369.00	5,530.07	5,695.97	5,866.85	=I21*1.05
Pre-paid expenses	-	-	-	-	-
Other	29,028.00	29,608.56	30,200.73	30,804.75	31,420.84

Figure 3.34: Inputting data with Excel formulas

Rosie now has to validate the numbers. If she feels these are accurate then she can send her forecasted balance sheet to the database. To do this she will click on the SAVE DATA button from the EPM Ribbon (see Figure 3.35).

Figure 3.35: Using the Save Data button from the EPM Ribbon

This process can be iterated upon until the forecast is finalized and all numbers are approved by the management.

Changing intersections to avoid overwriting input data

 Rosie can keep different versions of her financial forecasts by changing the **AU-DITTRAIL** dimension from the EPM Context, or by adding new members to the **CATEGORY** dimension before new versions are inputted. These are two common methodologies of how to maintain versions within a BPC model.

3.10 Summary

In this chapter we explored some key elements within the EPM Add-in and explored the EPM Pane, EPM Context, and the EPM Ribbon in detail. We outlined the basic rules that users should follow in order to build an EPM report. This will help them understand the basic principles of report building and to work in a way that makes maintenance and support easier.

Furthermore, we explained the key differences between a report and an input schedule and users should be able to identify when to use each one. In addition, different methodologies were explored to input data such as using EPMSave formulas, or using input schedules.

We discussed how leveraging the EPM formatting capabilities allows for corporate branding and usability enhancements. At this point, readers should have a solid understanding of the dynamic formatting capabilities that the EPM Add-in offers.

4. Data manager

The EPM Add-in displays more than just a single tab when you connect to a SAP Business Planning and Consolidation system. The EPM Ribbon we have been discussing thus far is the core ribbon within the EPM Add-in, however there is a second tab is just as important. By definition, the Data Manager tab is always rendered after logging into a BPC system but is grayed out when using other types of connections.

4.1   What is data manager?

Data manager is an Excel integrated interface that's intended for more advanced users and is located in the EPM Ribbon.

Data manager is specific to BPC

 It's important to note that the data manager tab is a planning and consolidation specific module that enhances the EPM Add-in features.

We refer to the data manager as an advanced user-focused tool because users have to be familiar with the way data intersections and dimensions work in order to take full advantage of the ETL capabilities that this tab brings into the Add-in (see Figure 4.1).

What is ETL?

 ETL stands for Extraction, Transformation and Loading.

The data manager tab offers several options to integrate data from various sources or to manipulate existing data thanks to its ETL capabilities. Common examples of manipulation functions or packages are currency conversions or consolidations. We will cover these in more detail later in this chapter with the extraction, transformation and loading data manager packages.

The data manager tab plays a critical role in any SAP Business Planning and Consolidation implementation.

Before moving on, let's go over some basic data manager terminology. The key term to get familiar with is *data manager package*. A data manager package is a logical unit of work that can be executed from the EPM Add-in. A package can load data, transform, or manipulate data as well as export data from the system.

This unit of work is called a package due to the heritage of the product itself. The original implementation of BPC was based on the Microsoft SQL Server Platform; this platform refers to an ETL process as a package. This terminology has continued on into all other versions of the BPC product.

The BPC data manager enables users to:

► Trigger data manager packages.

► Create and validate transformation files.

► Create and validate conversion files.

► View the status of data manager packages.

► Download, upload, and preview flat files from and to the SAP BPC server.

Figure 4.1: Data manager tab

4.1.1 Transformation files

Transformation files are Excel files stored in a central repository used by data manager packages with the sole purpose of interpreting data coming from external sources. This is a critical part of the BPC loading process. Transformation files drive core components within the BPC loading process

Transformation files are composed of three main sections:

► Options

► Mapping

► Conversion

The ***Options** section within a transformation file indicates the format and rules for how the system will read master or transactional data from an external source.

Exploring the options section

Sample *Options section of a transformation file:

*Options
FORMAT = DELIMITED
HEADER = YES
DELIMITER = ,
AMOUNTDECIMALPOINT = .
SKIP = 0
SKIPIF =
VALIDATERECORDS = YES
CREDIPOSITIVE = YES
MAXREJECTCOUNT = 200
ROUNDAMOUNT =

Using the options section in real-life scenarios

Users can specify several options depending on the case but the most widely used are as follows.

Changing the **DELIMITER** = Tab, space or comma depending on the file format that a user is trying to upload.

In case you have data quality issues you can set up a threshold of records the system will reject prior to interrupt a data load. **MAXREJECTCOUNT** = (for example 30).

Records can conditionally be skipped, an example would be filtering out specific text strings by using the **SKIPIF** keyword. If a data load should be setup to skip more than one text string, enter a pipe | in between each text string within the transformation file to indicate multiple conditions.

The **Mapping* section details how external data is mapped to specific BPC dimensions or properties.

All dimensions in a BPC model have to be mapped in the mapping section. Users can define hardcoded values by using the *NEWCOL(text_value) keyword. However, this rule only applies to dimensions, properties can be left blank.

Exploring the mapping section

Sample **Mapping* section of a transformation file used to load master data for the product dimension of Rosie's Lemonade.

*Mapping
ID=*COL(1)
BU=*COL(3)
SIZE=*COL(5)
SUGAR_FREE=*COL(6)
UOM=*COL(7)

The **Conversion* section of the transformation file is **optional** and it is used to indicate that the transformation file should call a conversion file.

Exploring the conversion section

Sample ***Conversion** section of a Transformation File used to convert units of measure for the product dimension.

*Conversion

UOM=UOM.xls

Figure 4.2: Sample transformation file

4.1.2 Conversion files

Conversion files are used to associate the external values coming from the data source to the equivalent internal values of BPC's dimension members. This is very useful especially during an implementation when you have to integrate data coming from several different sources or legacy systems that does not match the master data stored in BPC.

Conversion files are Excel files just like the transformation files, but they are only composed of three columns (see Figure 4.3).

▶ Internal

▶ External

▶ Formula

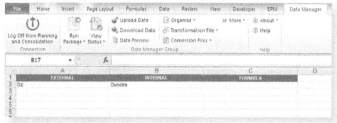

Figure 4.3: Sample conversion file

The internal column represents how the data is stored in BPC, while the external column defines how the data that's being loaded is stored. The formula column can be added if any calculations are required specifically when loading transactional data and you need to change the sign of an account. The formula column is optional and can be left blank.

Wildcards support

 Conversion files support the use of wild-cards in the external or internal columns. Users can make use of an asterisk (*) to indicate that the system is expecting any character.

Also, a question mark is also supported (?) and it's used to tell the system that it should expect any single character in a specific position. It can be used to re-place special characters for example **Rosie's**. If there's a member in the system that should be ig-nored during a load, users can make use of the *SKIP keyword to ignore it.

4.2 Data manager packages

Data manager packages are a set of instructions that users can define, or that are delivered by SAP out of the box to define inputs to an ETL process. Users can trigger these from the EPM Add-in Data Manager tab in the EPM Ribbon.

Among the capabilities that the data manager packages provide, users can find packages to copy, move, and clear data from and to specific models (see Figure 4.4).

Figure 4.4: Out of the box data manager packages

Data manager packages are very robust and powerful components that are layered on top of SQL Server Integration Services (SSIS) packages, or on top of SAP BW Process Chains and are specific to planning and consolidation connections. Our case study is based on BPC 10.1, version for SAP NetWeaver so we will focus on the latter of the two.

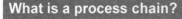

What is a process chain?

SAP BW process chains are a sequence of processes that wait in the background for an event to trigger them. These can be automated, monitored, visualized, centrally managed, or secured.

Each package behaves differently and can be modified from the ORGANIZE PACKAGE LIST dialog box from the Data Manager Tab; users can basically do any of the following activities to the packages within the Data Manager package groups (see Figure 4.5).

► Add a package.

► Modify a package.

► Remove a package.

► Copy a package.

► Move a package.

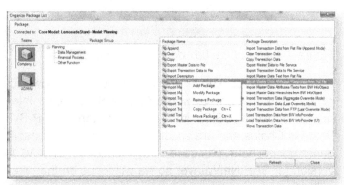

Figure 4.5: Organize package list options

► Data manager packages can be triggered indivi-
dually, or can be linked together by configuring package links.

► This is a simple task that follows the same rules
as triggering individual packages with a minor difference; they have to be executed sequentially. If
a precedent task fails the whole process will stop
executing.

Simplifying monthly operations with package links

 The following figure (see Figure 4.6) depicts a sample package link built for Rosie, or her super users, to execute on a monthly basis. It triggers three different tasks in sequence.

The package link depicted in Figure 4.6 was created to trigger three tasks:

▶ Master data loads for the product dimension.

▶ Transactional data load for actuals.

▶ Light optimize process.

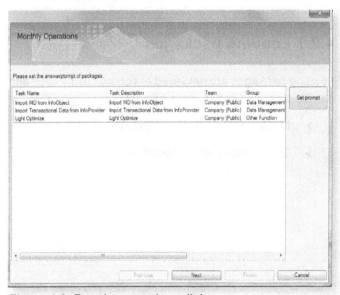

Figure 4.6: Running a package link

Light vs. Full optimize

 Light and full optimize are two SAP BPC specific process chains that are critical in any SAP Business Planning and Consolidation implementation. Its purpose is to close open requests and to compress the InfoCube. After this is complete, indexes are rebuilt to improve the model's performance.

The main difference between the two is that the latter reviews the SAP BPC data model for additional optimization. If this check finds that a more optimal Info-Cube structure is required, it creates a copy of the In-foCube, moves the data into the new optimized InfoCube, and deletes the old InfoCube.

4.2.1 Loading packages

Loading packages are delivered out of the box by SAP and can be classified in two main categories:

▶ Master data loading packages.

▶ Transactional data loading packages.

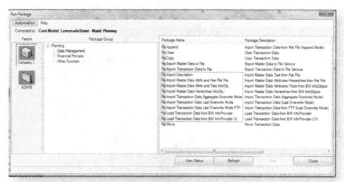

Figure 4.7: Loading packages

The EPM Add-in empowers business users to perform the loads by themselves, reducing the dependency on IT departments.

Triggering loading data manager packages is easy, intuitive, and requires minimum training for users to understand the basics and operate (see Figure 4.7).

4.2.1.1 Master data loading packages

Master data loading packages are used to import master data, descriptions, and hierarchies into planning and consolidation dimensions. They can be loaded from a flat file, or a BW InfoObject.

To trigger a master data load from a flat file, users must upload the file to the server first (see Figure 4.8).

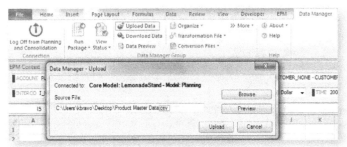

Figure 4.8: Uploading files to the server

Permitted formats when uploading flat files

You can only upload text files so, make sure you store your flat file as .csv or .txt before trying to upload it.

Uploading the product portfolio to BPC

Rosie would like to upload her product portfolio master data to the product dimension, but this data doesn't exist in any system or database. It only exists in an Excel spreadsheet controlled by Rosie's Lemonade Company's sales department.

After uploading this file to the server, she will use the SAP delivered **import master data attributes and texts from flat file** data manager package.

Loading packages can be triggered in two different modes:

▶ Update

▶ Overwrite

The main difference between these two modes is that the overwrite mode will delete all master data that's not posted against in the model. After completing this step, the data manager package will update the dimension with the information that's being pulled from the flat file. Another very common BPC dimension source are BW InfoObjects.

Update mode, on the other hand, will not delete any members. It will only update the changes made to the master data (see Figure 4.9).

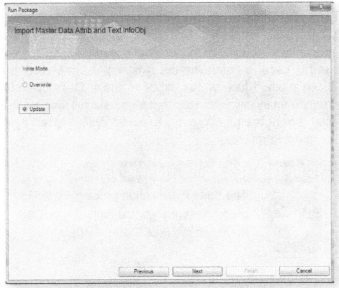

Figure 4.9: Different modes to load master data

4.2.1.2 Transactional data loading packages

BPC offers several packages to load transactional data out of the box accessible via the EPM Add-in.

Similar to master data load packages, the EPM Add-in allows users to upload transactional data from a flat file, or from a SAP BW InfoProvider.

If a user chooses the latter of the two options, transactional data can be loaded in two different ways:

▶ Full Upload

▶ Delta Upload

The main difference between the two is that delta uploads work based on request IDs. Simply put, a request ID represents a grouping of records that's read from the source and is used to determine the existence of new records. Each method has its own process chain. Delta uploads require an initialization step that triggers a full load on the first run. Subsequently, every execution will only pull new or updated records.

Setting up delta initializations

 The delta initialization process is configured from the organize menu in the Data Manager Tab (see Figure 4.10).

ORGANIZE • ORGANIZE DELTA INITIALIZATION Right Click then NEW.

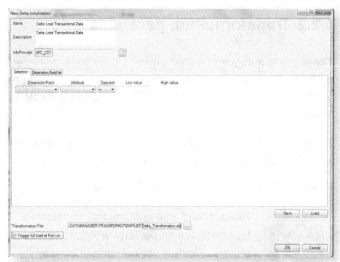

Figure 4.10: Setting up a new delta initialization

Keeping BW and BPC in sync

For Rosie's Lemonade Company, it's important to set up a delta load process to automate monthly operations since actuals are constantly changing and need to be reflected in the forecast. Regular delta loads will keep the BPC model in sync with the underlying BW data objects. Using delta loads will keep the run time for BW to BPC updates at a bare minimum, as only new or updated records will be loaded.

Rosie needs to specify a transformation file designed for transactional data loads.

As a general rule of thumb, it is best practice to trigger a full load on the first run if your target hasn't been loaded yet.

4.2.2 Transformation packages

There are a number of transformation packages delivered by SAP. Many of these data manager packages require additional configuration in the BPC web admin console to make them work.

The purpose of these packages is to enable users to transform the data stored in BPC in various ways.

> ### Real-life transformation examples
>
> Rosie could use a standard transformation package to perform allocations driven by Rosie's Lemonade Company's monthly sales to determine the profitability of a product or customer.
>
> She could also perform a series of what-if scenarios to calculate her COGS (Cost of Goods Sold) by multiplying the sales of a specific period against multiple variations of the costs derived from Rosie's Lemonade bills of materials.

Transformations packages can drive all types of different calculations. BPC has an embedded scripting language that is used to manipulate plan and forecast data. Script logic programs can perform all sorts of calculations, ranging from arithmetic operations to complex allocation operations. Script logic calculations are executed from standard SAP packages delivered with BPC.

What is Script Logic?

 Script Logic (also known as K2 logic) utilizes SQL like commands and MDX to perform calculations on planning and consolidation data.

Users can create files called logic scripts (.LGF extension) that contain a series of instructions split in three sections (scoping, body/code and database commits). Logic scripts provide flexibility to advanced users to perform model-specific calculations.

There are a series of additional transformations that SAP delivers with standard BPC installations. These out of the box calculations are referred to as business rules (see Figure 4.11).

▶ Allocations

▶ FX restatements

▶ Intercompany eliminations

▶ Legal consolidations

▶ Balance carry forward

▶ Ownership calculations

▶ Account calculations

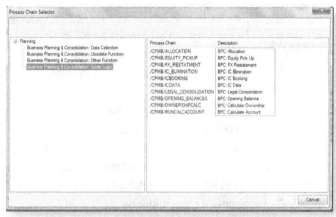

Figure 4.11: Transformation data manager packages

4.2.3 Extraction packages

Another useful feature that the data manager provides is the ability to perform extractions from data that's stored in BPC and export it for use in downstream systems (see Figure 4.12).

SAP's out of the box extraction data manager packages make possible to export this data:

▶ To application servers

▶ To flat files

▶ Via retraction Business Add-ins or BAdI's

What is a BADI?

Business Add-ins, or BADIs, are SAP programming enhancements based on ABAP Objects. BAdI's are the new methodology that SAP employs to extend standard functionality to meet complex sets of customer requirements.

Figure 4.12: Extraction data manager packages

Real-life retraction example

Rosie's Lemonade Company could use the retraction BADI to pull month-end specific adjustments, made directly in BPC with an input schedule, with the purpose of sending them to their BW and ERP systems to keep their systems landscape in sync.

4.3   Data manager prompts

The core function of the data manager package is to expose ETL processes to business users through an easy to consume interface. Data manager prompts are elements woven together that make up the business user interface.

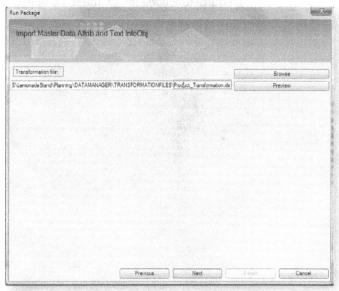

Figure 4.13: Data manager prompts

User selections are cached in a local file

 The EPM Add-in automatically stores the history of each prompt value for the last run on a Local .XML file called DMUserSelection.xml. Users can use this file to store predefined prompt values.

You can customize the data manager package prompts via dynamic scripting, we will cover this in more detail in the next section of this chapter (see section 4.4).

4.4   Advanced package script editor

The advanced package script editor is a very powerful tool that users can leverage to customize data manager packages.

The advanced package script editor is commonly used to simplify data entry by hardcoding values into the packages. This is very useful when dealing with multiple data manager prompts.

Providing additional instructions to guide users through the process of running data manager packages is another core ability that the advanced package script editor enables.

The anatomy of a data manager package

 To access the advanced package script editor, you have to modify a data manager package from the ORGANIZE PACKAGE LIST button in the DATA MANAGER tab.
Then, right click the MODIFY PACKAGE option and then click on the MODIFY SCRIPT Button (see Figure 4.14).

Figure 4.14: Modify script button

In addition to enhancing the end-user experience, the advanced script editor is used to map data entered in the prompts to the back-end.

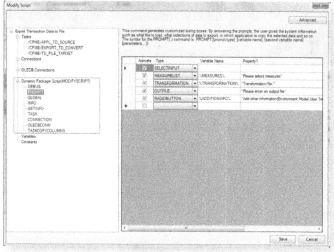

Figure 4.15: Dynamic package script editor

Users can interact with the dynamic package editor directly from the screen shown above.

There's also an advanced mode that allows users to modify the scripts directly bypassing the standard UI by clicking the Aᴅᴠᴀɴᴄᴇᴅ button in the top right corner (see Figu-re 4.15) to display the actual script as depicted in Figure 4.16.

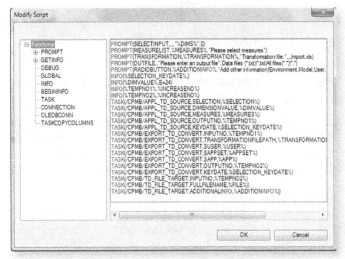

Figure 4.16: Dynamic package scripting

The three main functions that users need to be familiar with to modify a data manager package are:

▶ PROMPT

▶ INFO

▶ TASK

PROMPT commands control input selections allowing users to pass selections or variable inputs to data mana-ger packages.

INFO commands are non-executable instructions that al-low users to set values for the variables that a data mana-ger package expects.

TASK commands map the values collected by the PROMPT and INFO commands to variables within backend SAP BW process chain variants.

4.5 Logging and monitoring

Monitoring is a critical activity when running data manager packages.

Monitoring options

Monitoring can be done directly from data manager tab, or from the backend in transactions SM66 or SM37. The aforementioned transactions are only relevant for BPC, version for SAP NetWeaver.

Every single data manager package can be monitored during its execution. The ability to view the status of a running or completed data manager package is accessible from the EPM Add-in's data manager ribbon. The logging functionality is extremely user friendly and intuitive to use. To access view status monitoring, users just have to click on the VIEW STATUS button from the data manager tab or from the run package window (see Figure 4.17).

Figure 4.17: View status button in the data manager tab

It's important that users learn how to navigate to and decipher the different statuses that the monitoring tool displays so that they can quickly identify problems while running

Data Manager Packages (see Figure 4.18).

The different statuses that the DATA MANAGER - VIEW STATUS monitoring tool can provide are:

► Running

► Succeeded

► Failed

► Warning

The EPM Add-in has a very robust logging functionality that can be used to troubleshoot several problems ranging from errors in (see Figure 4.19):

► Master data loads

► Transactional data loads

► Script logic executions

► Optimizations

► Etc.

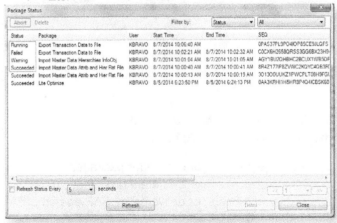

Figure 4.18: Data Manager Package Status

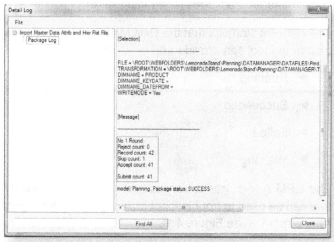

Figure 4.19: Data manager package logs

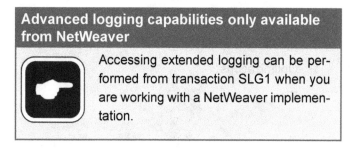

Advanced logging capabilities only available from NetWeaver

Accessing extended logging can be performed from transaction SLG1 when you are working with a NetWeaver implementation.

4.6 Summary

In this chapter users gained an understanding of transformation and conversion file basics.

Likewise, we defined data manager packages as a set of work items used to achieve different tasks that can be customized by end users, or delivered by SAP as part of the standard functionality.

With this information, it is expected that users understand how to work with these packages to close the gaps in order to comply with different client requirements.

After categorizing each package into three main categories (extract, transform and load), users should feel comfortable with deciding when to use each one.

Additionally, we explored complex capabilities like the advanced dynamic editor, which allows users to customize data manager packages to achieve different tasks that are not delivered out of the box.

Finally, you have learned more about how to work with the logging and monitoring capabilities that the Add-in provides. During that time, we talked about different ways to analyze and interpret the results that a data manager package can output that could potentially help whith performing basic troubleshooting.

5. Advanced features

The EPM Add-in is a very user-friendly tool that financial users like because they are familiar with the Excel functionality. This is a great selling point because users can still work with pivot tables, conditional formatting, filtering, Excel formulas, etc. The add-in is easy to learn and becomes easier to operate after working with it a few times.

There are multiple avenues that expert users can leverage to customize the EPM Add-in that range from modifying the underlying XML configuration files, to using the advanced formatting features of the EPM Formatting sheet and using out-of-the box EPM APIs in VBA.

5.1   Using VBA within the EPMAddin

Microsoft Excel is an extremely powerful tool that users can use to transform and present data. However, there are situations where the available User Interface (UI) functionality isn't enough, especially when executing repetitive tasks. This is where VBA comes into play.

VBA is an event-driven programming language that works by executing step-by-step instructions written in Visual Basic. Because it's embedded in Excel, EPM users can take advantage of it and leverage the APIs that were built by SAP to enrich their reports and add functionality.

EPM API support

Despite the fact that the EPM Add-in works for PowerPoint, Word, and Excel, the APIs are only supported in Excel.

In earlier versions of the add-in, SAP delivered preconfigured macros called menu commands.

Menu commands

One of the most used menu commands was the MNU_eDATA_RUNPACKAGE in BPC 7.x.
This Menu command allowed users to run a data manager package by clicking a button directly from the Excel sheet.

Menu commands were used to trigger specific EV functions. Users could invoke these commands by assigning them to VBA macros, or by using the "=EvMNU" formula. However, this changed with the 10.x release.

With the new release, it became mandatory to include the FPMXLClient Library as a reference. After referencing the library, users can access the EPMAddInAutomation and EPMAddInDMAutomation classes and their associated functions to write macros.

Adding the FPMXLClient library as a reference

 To make the FPMXLClient library available, users need to go to the Top Menu Bar • TOOLS • REFERENCES. Check the box to the left of the FPMXLClient Library and then click OK (see Figure 5.1)

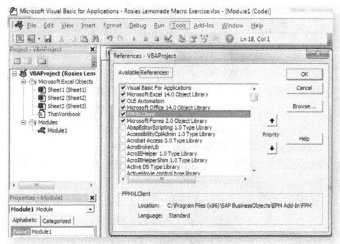

Figure 5.1: Adding FPMXLClient library as a reference

This feature is especially helpful to develop business friendly reports for those users that want to avoid the EPM Add-in Ribbon.

Real-life scenarios

 Rosie would like to add a button to one of her planning input schedules that allows her to trigger a 5% increase in sales.

She wants to place this button in the upper left corner of the report to avoid going through the run package menu every time she wants to trigger this package. After enabling the developer tab in Excel and adding a button to the spreadsheet, she built a macro as depicted in Figure 5.2 that triggers the allocation package calling her 5% increase logic script file. To achieve this, she's calling a function called Data-ManagerOpenRunPackageDialog, which displays the entire catalog of data manager packages. Another approach would be to use the DataManagerRunPackage function and to pass the name of the data manager package as the first argument ("Allocation"), the name of the package group in which this package is located ("Financial Process") and leaving the Team ID empty because this is located in the company public folder. Rosie also configured two sub-functions in the same VBA module to refresh the active sheet and to call the spread planning function.

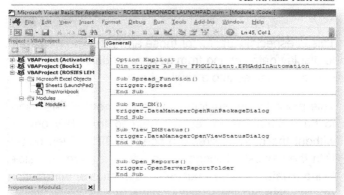

Figure 5.2: Run a data manager package with VBA

All VBA functions can be triggered with specific EPM events, some of the most widely used in implementations are as follows:

- ▶ BEFORE_CONTEXTCHANGE

- ▶ AFTER_CONTEXTCHANGE

- ▶ BEFORE_REFRESH

- ▶ AFTER_REFRESH

- ▶ BEFORE_SAVE

- ▶ AFTER_SAVE

5.2 Multi-source reporting

One of the most powerful features that the add-in offers is the power of performing multi-source reporting. Users can have multiple reports in an Excel sheet and each one of them can be connected to different data sources (connections).

This is especially useful for those analysts who may want to display data coming from several models or data sources, consolidated into a single sheet.

This powerful but seldom-used component allows users to build consolidated reports sourced from BW objects without the need to create models in BPC. Even better, with the newest additions to the add-in it's even possible to input data by using input enabled queries or Information Access, INA providers (see Figure 5.3).

Figure 5.3: Setting up a connection to an input enabled query

Each connection is defined from the EPM Pane under the Data Connection drop box (see Figure 5.4 and Figure 5.5).

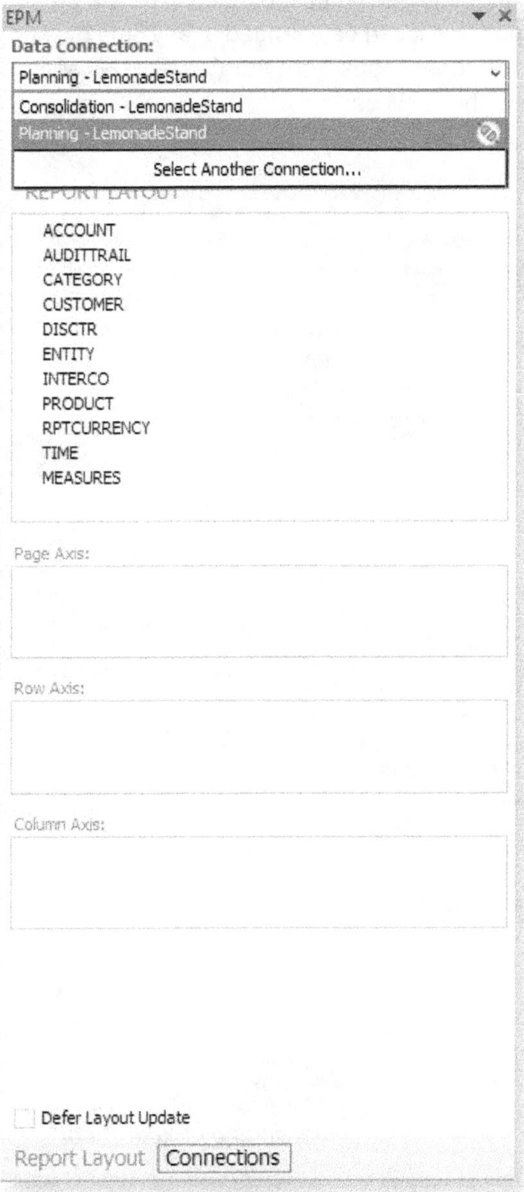

Figure 5.4: Selecting a connection for a new report

We recommend setting the connection before creating the new report, but it can be changed at any time by managing the active connections from the CONNECTIONS MENU in the bottom of the EPM pane.

Figure 5.5: Specific connections by Excel sheet

Sharing axes between reports from different sources is also permitted. This is configured from the report editor by selecting either the row or the column axes as Shared (see Figure 5.6).

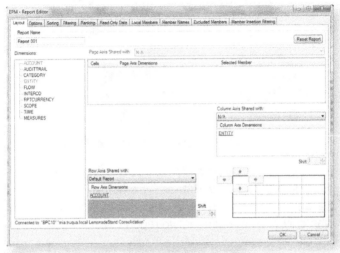

Figure 5.6: Sharing axes between reports

Users have to take into account that sharing axes is resource intensive and can take a toll on the report's performance.

5.3   Advanced formatting

Thanks to Excel's integration with the EPM Add-in, creating beautiful reports is easy.

By leveraging macros, charts, buttons, forms, and pictures Rosie's EPM reports now look amazing. This makes the end-user experience more complete and steps reports up a notch (see Figure 5.7).

Figure 5.7: Creating beautiful reports directly from Excel

Rosie even configured a launch board for those users who struggle with the EPM Ribbon. This helped her to reduce the amount of training for a considerable amount of users who only work with one or two reports to display data.

In Rosie's experience, having visually appealing and functional reports helped to facilitate, and also to accelerate, user adoption.

In some cases, applying advanced formatting features to reports can fulfill additional requirements.

One of the most common advanced formatting use cases is the incorporation of dynamic scaling into reports.

Using the EPMScaleData formula

 The EPM function EPMScaleData enables users to reference a cell in an EPM report that can be referenced to control the scaling displayed in a report.

This function basically takes every amount within a cell and divides it by the scaling factor. Thanks to this feature users are able to display their financials in hundreds, thousands, or millions with minor effort.

Scaling can be configured directly from the EPM Add-in and applied to a specific cell. This can also be done by overriding the content for the desired members in the column and row axes in the EPM formatting sheet (see Figure 5.8).

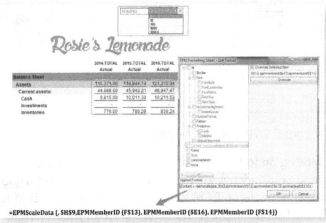

=EPMScaleData (, H9,EPMMemberID (F$13), EPMMemberID ($E16), EPMMemberID (F$14))

Figure 5.8: Using a dropdown menu to configure scaling

121

> ## Using content overridecould impact performance
>
> Avoid over using the content override function. The EPM Add-in retrieves data in two steps instead of just one causing performance detriments in some cases (writing + calculation).

To set up dynamic scaling, we need to access the EPM FORMATTING SHEET – CELL FORMAT window. In order to override the contents of the report you need to double click any of the cells in the **Use** column as depicted by Figure 5.9. By default all the values in this column are set to ALL.

Figure 5.9: Accessing the cell format menu

Moving on to the next advanced formatting best practice, report builders have to keep in mind that it is always a good idea to create an EPM formatting sheet for each EPM report. This will improve the performance of your reports.

Handle conditional formatting with caution

 The conditional formatting functionality was introduced with Excel 1997 and has been around for years allowing users to apply dynamic formats to workbooks depending on the value of a cell or a formula. While it performs well in most cases, it can be resource intensive on reports that display large amounts of data. As a result, avoid using conditional formatting in your EPM formatting sheet. Although Excel's formatting capabilities are highly robust, the performance impact of using conditional formatting along with the EPM formatting sheet can degrade performance due to the evaluation of every single cell while applying your formatting rules.

5.4   Troubleshooting EPM Addin issues

Troubleshooting the EPM Add-in can be a complex task, but there are some standard features built in the EPM Ribbon along with some third-party tools that can help make this task easier.

Users can go to the MORE button in the EPM Ribbon and click on the LOG... button. This will bring a pop up window that displays some technical data that can be useful for troubleshooting simple EPM errors.

It's also possible to enhance the logging capabilities by modifying the FPMXLClient.dll-ExcelLogConfig.xml file.

In this file, there's a section where logging levels are defined.

The first thing that must be modified in the XML file is the EXCLUSIVE LOCK values, all of them need to be replaced by MINIMAL LOCK instead. This setting controls the behavior of the write/delete capabilities that the EPM Add-in has over the log files. If it's set to EXCLUSIVE LOCK, then the add-in cannot modify nor delete the log until Excel is closed (see Figure 5.10).

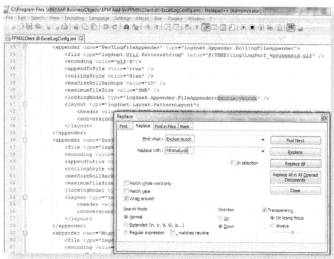

Figure 5.10: Changing the locking behavior of EPM logs

The next step is to find and modify the following level values for each one of the logs that the EPM Add-in records.

This list contains the different log files and their default level values.

▶ Migration – ALL

▶ Log – ERROR

▶ Trace – ERROR

▶ Performance Log – ERROR

▶ Performance Trace - ERROR

The possible level values that can be set are (see Figure 5.11):

▶ ALL

▶ ALERT

▶ ERROR

▶ WARN

▶ NOTICE

▶ INFO

▶ DEBUG

▶ TRACE

▶ VERBOSE

```xml
<logger name="Log.FPMXLClient.Migration">
    <level value="ALL" />
    <appender-ref ref="MigrationLogFileAppender" />
</logger>
<logger name="Log">
    <level value="ERROR" />
    <appender-ref ref="DefaultLogFileAppender" />
</logger>
<logger name="Trace">
    <level value="ERROR" />
    <appender-ref ref="DefaultTraceFileAppender" />
</logger>
<logger name="Log.Performance">
    <level value="ERROR" />
    <appender-ref ref="PerfLogFileAppender" />
</logger>
<logger name="Trace.Performance">
    <level value="ERROR" />
    <appender-ref ref="PerfTraceFileAppender" />
</logger>
<logger name="Recorder">
    <level value="ALL" />
</logger>
```

Figure 5.11: Changing the level of detail for the EPM Logs

Excluding the first value in the list (ALL), the rest are based on priorities that follow a hierarchical order; where ALERT is priority 1, ERROR is priority 2, and so on.

Location of the EPM log files

 Logs are stored in the following path:
C:\Users\%username%\AppData\Local\Temp\log
These logs should be used to analyze EPM errors.

One of the most common issues with the EPM Add-in is that after a critical error where Excel crashes, Microsoft Office displays a prompt when you try to open the application again asking for permission to disable the EPM Add-in. If users are not careful when answering this prompt, they will deactivate it and cause the EPM tabs to disappear from Excel.

To re-enable the EPM Add-in users must go into EXCEL OPTIONS • ADD-INS • DISABLED ADD-INS and then select EPM ADD-IN FOR MICROSOFT OFFICE • Click OK and close and launch Excel again (see Figure 5.12).

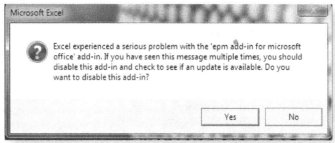

Figure 5.12: How to avoid Microsoft Excel from disabling the EPM Add-in

Another common issue within the EPM Add-in occurs when a user tries to display a report with too many rows or columns. In this situation, the Add-in displays an error stating that the maximum number of tuples has been reached (see Figure 5.13).

What is a tuple?

A tuple is an ordered collection of one or more members in a dimension used to define a slice of data from a cube. In the EPM space, these are written in MDX language.

For example:
([Time].[PARENTH1].[2014.01], [Product].
[PARENTH1].[LEMONADE])

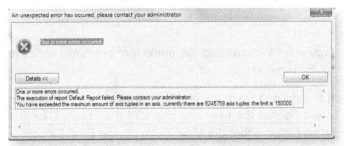

Figure 5.13: Exceeding the number of permitted tuples in a EPM report

When this error occurs, the report is most likely trying to pull too much data at once and the report should be analyzed. If for some reason there's an absolute need to pull this number of records, it is possible to change a setting in the FPMXLClient.ddl.config file and increase the value of the LimitAmountAxisTupleInAxis (see Figure 5.14).

127

Default setting of the LimitAmountAxisTupleInAxis

The default value of LimitAmountAxisTupleInAxis is 150,000.

```
<add key="ClientSettingsProvider.ServiceUri" value="" />
<add key="Log4NetEXCELInitFile" value="./FPMXLClient.dll-ExcelLogConfig.xml"/>
<add key="Log4NetWINWORDInitFile" value="./FPMXLClient.dll-WordLogConfig.xml"/>
<add key="Log4NetPOWERPNTInitFile" value="./FPMXLClient.dll-PowerPointLogConfig.xml"/>
<add key="AccessControl" value="true"/>
<add key="SkipLoadingWhenEmbedded" value="false"/>
<add key="UploadChunkSize" value="262144"/>
<add key="LimitAmountAxisTupleInAxis" value="150000"/>
<add key="LimitToAsymmetric" value="50000"/>
<add key="LimitTDHCountInCache" value="3"/>
<add key="SaveDynAxisIfStaticAxisLengthExceed" value="2000"/>
<add key="SmartQueryEngineThreshold" value="5"/>
<add key="SmartQueryEngineMaxAxisRequests" value="1"/>
<add key="SmartQueryEngineMaxTupleByCellRequest" value="20000"/>
<add key="SmartReportValueWrittingMinBlockSize" value="500"/>
<add key="SmartReportValueWrittingMaxBlockSize" value="10000"/>
<add key="SmartReportValueWrittingMinBlockRowsRatio" value="10"/>
<add key="AutoActiveEPMSheet" value="false"/>
```

Figure 5.14: Increasing the amount of permitted tuples in an EPM report

If this doesn't solve the problem, another possible reason could be that the user has checked the FREEZE DATA REFRESH button under the MORE button in the EPM Ribbon.

This option overwrites the suppression settings configured in the sheet options menu. This forces the report to bring back all the member of the dimensions selected on the rows or columns of the report.

Fiddler is a freeware third-party debugging application used to capture HTTP and HTTPS traffic. This tool can be very useful for troubleshooting errors within the EPM Add-in. Fiddler can also be used to analyze performance issues. A core function within Fiddler is the ability to display the size of each request, its content, and the time spent on each layer of transmission/reception process.

The information retrieved by Fiddler can easily be displayed in different formats and can be analyzed by someone with a web-oriented technical background (see Figure 5.15).

Figure 5.15: Third party tools: Fiddler overview

A very common error occurs when users have a combination of base level members and parents in the same input schedule (see Figure 5.16).

Rosie's Lemonade

	2014.DEC Actual	2015.DEC Actual	2016.DEC Actual	2017.DEC Actual	2018.DEC FCST 1+11	2018.TOTAL FCST 1+11
Balance Sheet						
Assets	116,371.00	118,844.74	121,372.34	123,955.02	126,434.12	126,434.12
Current assets:	44,986.00	45,949.21	46,947.47	47,993.74	49,156.81	49,156.81
Cash	9,815.00	10,011.30	10,211.53	10,415.76	10,624.07	10,624.07
Investments	-	-	-	-	-	-
Inventories	776.00	799.28	839.24	906.38	951.70	951.70

Figure 5.16: Mixing base and node level members in a single EPM report

This scenario will always return a combination of accepted and rejected records on every data submission. The rejected records are generated because there's data trying being saved in a calculated member. Calculated members are not input ready (see Figure 5.17).

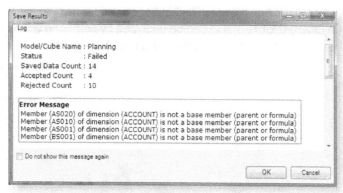

Figure 5.17: Inputting data to node level members

To solve this issue end users have to enable the following option from the USER OPTIONS MENU • OTHERS • UNCHECK the SEND PARENT DATA TO THE SERVER ON SAVE DATA. By unchecking this option, the add-in will stop sending the values displayed on the parents and the error will go away (see Figure 5.18).

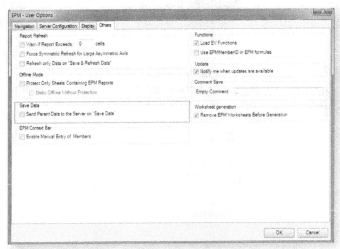

Figure 5.18: Solving the sending data to parent level nodes error

5.5 SAP Dashboards integration

From the EPM Ribbon users can insert flash objects into reports.

5.5.1 But, what is a flash object?

When we talk about flash objects in the EPM Add-in space, we are talking about powerful and graphical representations of a report commonly referred to as dashboards.

Users need to create these dashboards from SAP BusinessObjects Dashboard Design and they can be later inserted in Microsoft Office Excel, Word, or PowerPoint using the add-in.

To be able to create dashboards pulling data from the EPM suite, a special connector called the EPM Connector is needed.

The connector has to be installed in SAP BusinessObjects Dashboards (formerly known as Xcelsius) from the File Menu as an Add-on (see Figure 5.19).

Figure 5.19: Installing the EPM Connector

What is the EPM Connector?

 The EPM Connector is a component that is part of the EPM Add-in (included with the installation as of Service Pack 13). It is installed directly in the SAP BusinessObjects Dashboard Design as an add-in. The target audience for this connector is more technical than the EPM Add-in, it requires that the operator is familiar with the SAP Dashboards Design application and it's functionality. Users can find the EPMConnector.xls file in the following location C:\Program Files (x86)\SAP BusinessObjects\EPM Add-In\EPMConnector\EPMConnector.xls.

The EPM Connector offers two main benefits of integration with the EPM Add-in:

▶ The ability to display visually appealing dashboards within reports and the ability to link these embedded dashboards to the EPM context for live data updates.

▶ The write-back capability enabling end users to modify transactional data straight from the dashboard and in real time.

To setup a connection using the EPM Connector, first we need to create a report with the data structure that we want to leverage for our dashboard. This report must be created from the SAP BusinessObjects Dashboards Excel window using the EPM Add-in or Extended Analytics Analyzer (see Figure 5.20).

		Column Axis			
	Actual	Actual	Actual	Actual	FCST 1+11
Row Axis	2014.DEC	2015.DEC	2016.DEC	2017.DEC	2018.DEC
Cash	9,815.00	10,011.30	10,211.53	10,415.76	10,624.07
Inventories	776.00	799.28	839.24	906.38	951.70
Accounts receivable	5,369.00	5,530.07	5,695.97	5,866.85	6,160.19
Other	29,028.00	29,608.56	30,200.73	30,804.75	31,420.84

Page Axis

PRODUCT
DISCTR
CUSTOMER

Figure 5.20: Base report to be used as a data source

▶ To get all the components that we need to setup an EPM Connector connection we need to talk about a very special XML function.

▶ The =GetReportDefinition() function is used to retrieve the definition of the report that will be used as the data source for our dashboards. Using this function is mandatory because it is required by the EPM Connector to establish a connection.

Understanding the =GetReportDefinition()

Sample string returned by the =GetReportDefinition() function:

<Structure><Report Name="Default Report" SheetName="Sheet1" MDX="SELECT NON EMPTY {([/CPMB/A3DFJIN]. [ACTUAL], [/CPMB/A3D9DT2].[2014.12]), ([/CPMB/A3DFJIN].[ACTUAL], [/CPMB/A3D9DT2]. [2015.12]),([/CPMB/A3DFJIN].[ACTUAL], [/CPMB/ A3D9DT2].[2016.12]),([/CPMB/A3DFJIN].[ACTUAL], [/CPMB/A3D9DT2].[2017.12]),([/CPMB/A3DFJIN]. [FCST_1_11], [/CPMB/A3D9DT2].[2018.12])}ON COLUMNS ...

This function can work without passing any arguments (by leaving the parentheses empty). If this is the case, it identifies the default report. If an end user creates another report on the same sheet, they must re-enter the function to retrieve the new definition. However, this time they have to include the name of the report inside the parentheses and with quotation marks.

Using the =GetReportDefinition() with more than one report

Here are some examples of how to use the =GetReportDefinition() function: =GetReportDefinition("Report001") or =GetReportDefinition("Report000") to retrieve the different definitions for two reports defined in the same sheet.

To setup a connection users have to click on the top menu DATA and then select CONNECTIONS (or use the shortcut Ctrl + M) and select the EPM CONNECTOR form the drop down list (see Figure 5.21).

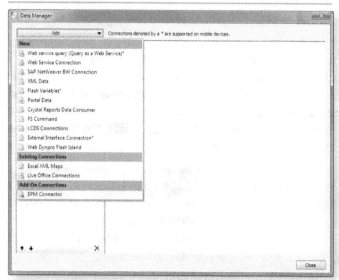

Figure 5.21: Setting up the EPM Connector

Once complete, we need to select the application and operation that we want to perform with the EPM Connector. We will leverage the "=GetReportDefinition()" formula and we will specify an output range for our dashboard (see Figure 5.22).

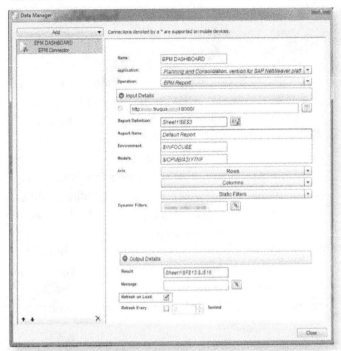

Figure 5.22: Configuring an EPM Connector connection

After doing this, we can start working on our dashboard keeping in mind that we need to insert a refresh button. Being able to setup a retrieve via the EPM Connector is a critical part of keeping our dashboard in sync. This can be scheduled so the refresh occurs every x seconds, or on-demand by pressing a button.

This brief example shows how the integration between the EPM Add-in and dashboards work. It is important that users know how to design dashboards in order to take full advantage of this integration feature and to perform advanced customizations.

Integrating the EPM Add-in with BO Dashboards at Rosie's Lemonade

 Rosie wants to analyze the composition of her current assets in a graphical manner that is pleasing to look at. She asked her BusinessObjects team to design a sample dashboard.

With this dashboard, Rosie realized that she could complement her executive reports using simple forms of analysis to showcase several years of information in a visually pleasing manner.

Rosie was very excited about the possibility of leveraging advanced features in the future to input and modify her forecast by making the changes directly in an executive dashboard to perform what-if scenarios (see Figure 5.23).

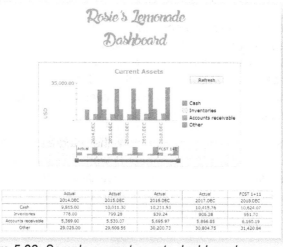

	Actual	Actual	Actual	Actual	FCST 1+11
	2014.DEC	2015.DEC	2016.DEC	2017.DEC	2018.DEC
Cash	9,815.00	10,011.30	10,211.53	10,415.76	10,624.07
Inventories	776.00	799.28	839.24	906.38	951.70
Accounts receivable	5,369.00	5,530.07	5,695.97	5,866.85	6,160.19
Other	29,026.00	29,606.55	30,200.73	30,804.75	31,420.84

Figure 5.23: Sample current assets dashboard

5.6   Summary

In this chapter, we looked at the advanced features that the EPM Add-in offers including integrating VBA macros with the EPM FPMXL library, performing multi-source reporting, creating beautiful reports leveraging advanced formatting techniques, and troubleshooting the EPM Add-in.

With these tools, it is expected that end users and report builders have a deeper understanding of the kind of reports that can be built using the add-in.

Also, users can learn from the scenarios depicted above to avoid spending hours trying to troubleshoot common errors. In addition, we talked about troubleshooting techniques and third party software solutions that can help to debug complex errors or analyze and fine tune performance settings.

Likewise, Rosie was able to build a launchpad to accelerate user adoption and to facilitate learning for junior analysts without any EPM training.

Finally, we also covered integration with dashboards, the EPM Connector, and flash objects. Advanced report builders with a solid knowledge of SAP BusinessObjects Dashboards can leverage these features to deliver visually stunning reports aimed for executives to facilitate decision-making.

6. Extending the EPM AddIn

When implementing BPC and rolling out the EPM Add-in there are typically two dichotomies that customers fall into. Those who want to see fewer features within the EPM Ribbon, and those who want to add more functionality to it. BPC and the EPM Add-in offer unprecedented extensibility features from the backend to the EPM frontend client.

In this chapter, we will address different options to enhance and extend the EPM Add-in.

We will cover the basics for each option, along with some examples to showcase distinct features that advanced users can leverage.

In addition, end users may want to customize the EPM Add-in to make some features more accessible. After all, the add-in offers a great deal of options to customize the frontend display and behavior. Having said that, there are a series of steps required to enable custom ribbon functions or to simplify the existing ribbon by removing standard buttons from the standard ribbon.

6.1 Customizing the EPM Addin

The EPM Add-in offers a wide range of features and functions that are accessible from the EPM Ribbon. In many organizations, the number of functions is overwhelming and there is a desire to remove some of the buttons or sections limiting the functions available. Contrarily, some customers feel that the ribbon could be extended to support new functionality or to augment existing processes.

By creating an XML file, users can create extensions to customize the EPM Ribbon. It is possible to define new buttons, create shortcuts to the most used functions, or set up menus and submenus.

Where to save the RibbonXML.xml file

 To customize the EPM Ribbon advanced users have to create an XML file called RibbonXML.xml and save it in the following location:

\%username%\AppData\Local\EPMOfficeClient\

Looking back at our business case, Rosie wanted to make the ACTIVATE MEMBER RECOGNITION option (located in of the sheet options menu) more accessible.. Since most of her analysts use this function on a daily basis, she decided to create her own button in the EPM Ribbon and push it to the end users as part of the installation process.

The XML file in Figure 6.1 depicts a series of instructions to tell the EPM Ribbon how to manage Rosie's new custom extension.

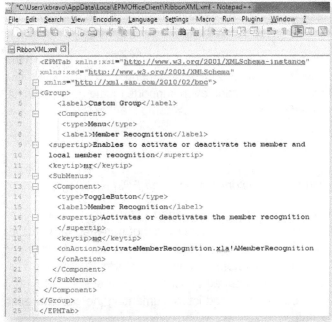

Figure 6.1: Creating a custom button for the EPM Ribbon

The main elements that were used to define the component depicted in Figure 6.1 are:

- ▶ <Group>

- ▶ <label>

- ▶ <Component>

- ▶ <type>

- ▶ <keytip>

- ▶ <onAction>

- ▶ <onPressed>

- ▶ <isEnabled>

143

Each one of these elements defines an object or action used to control the behavior of our newly created extension in the EPM Ribbon.

The previous exercise will display a custom menu with the active member recognition submenu. As you can see, this type of customization even supports toggle buttons, which are defined with the <type> component in the XML.

Figure 6.2: Custom menus in the EPM Ribbon

Customizing is a double-edged sword; while some clients might love or need a specific set of non-standard functionality there is always the drawback of having to maintain and support customizations longer term. If a system customization is required ensure that your system integrator (SI) does a very good job documenting the customization both functionally and technically.

General impacts to custom developments

 With the introduction of new service packs, clients have to keep in mind that their customizations might be impacted, just like any other custom development.

Fortunately, all of these extensions are built leveraging XML and VBA, two very popular programming languages that are easy to learn and that many people already know. This extensibility option meets a good set of requirements, however for more complex requirements there are other options.

In addition to ribbon customization via XML, the ability to highly customize the frontend or customer interaction can be extended via a visual studio ribbon project. To develop an extension for the EPM Ribbon with Visual Studio, developers will need to create and empty library class (.dll) and name it in a way so that it ends with 'RibbonExtension.dll'.

There are 4 main libraries that need to be added to the project:

► FPMXLClient.RibbonUtilies.dll

► stdole.dll

► Office.dll V12

► System.ComponentModel.Composition.dll

IEpmRibbonExtensibility is a required interface that needs to be added to the project class. After this, the project needs to be compiled and saved   to the folder that contains all the EPM .dlls (C:\Program Files (x86)\SAP BusinessObjects\EPM Add-in). The extension will be loaded the next time you open Microsoft Office Excel, Word, or PowerPoint.

Finally, there is another approach to customize the EPM Ribbon. This will allow buttons and other elements of the ribbon to be shown, hidden, or changed. This can be achieved by modifying the FPMXLClientPreference.XLM file.

Where can I find the EPMXLClientPreference. XLM file?

The EPMXLClientPreference.XLM file is located   in: C:\Users\kbravo\AppData\Local\EPMOfficeClient\FPMXLClientPreference.XLM

The XML file structure is very simple to understand.

Almost every setting can be modified simply by toggling the true / false values (see Figure 6.3).

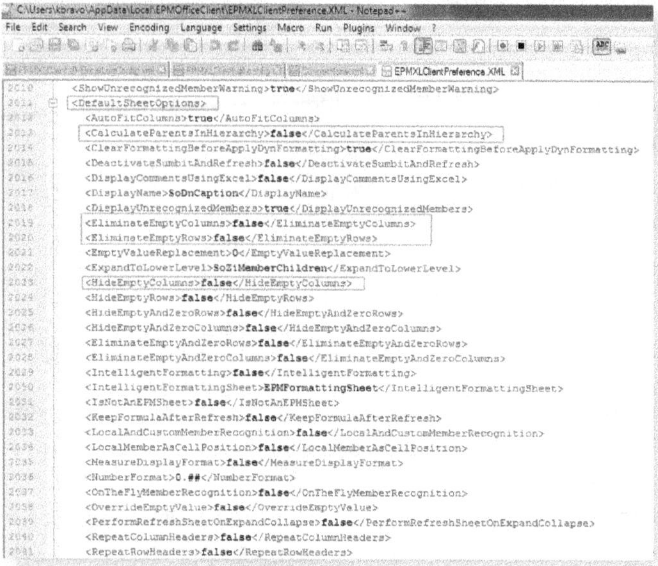

```
<ShowUnrecognizedMemberWarning>true</ShowUnrecognizedMemberWarning>
<DefaultSheetOptions>
  <AutoFitColumns>true</AutoFitColumns>
  <CalculateParentsInHierarchy>false</CalculateParentsInHierarchy>
  <ClearFormattingBeforeApplyDynFormatting>true</ClearFormattingBeforeApplyDynFormatting>
  <DeactivateSumbitAndRefresh>false</DeactivateSumbitAndRefresh>
  <DisplayCommentsUsingExcel>false</DisplayCommentsUsingExcel>
  <DisplayName>SoDnCaption</DisplayName>
  <DisplayUnrecognizedMembers>true</DisplayUnrecognizedMembers>
  <EliminateEmptyColumns>false</EliminateEmptyColumns>
  <EliminateEmptyRows>false</EliminateEmptyRows>
  <EmptyValueReplacement>0</EmptyValueReplacement>
  <ExpandToLowerLevel>SoZiMemberChildren</ExpandToLowerLevel>
  <HideEmptyColumns>false</HideEmptyColumns>
  <HideEmptyRows>false</HideEmptyRows>
  <HideEmptyAndZeroRows>false</HideEmptyAndZeroRows>
  <HideEmptyAndZeroColumns>false</HideEmptyAndZeroColumns>
  <EliminateEmptyAndZeroRows>false</EliminateEmptyAndZeroRows>
  <EliminateEmptyAndZeroColumns>false</EliminateEmptyAndZeroColumns>
  <IntelligentFormatting>false</IntelligentFormatting>
  <IntelligentFormattingSheet>EPMFormattingSheet</IntelligentFormattingSheet>
  <IsNotAnEPMSheet>false</IsNotAnEPMSheet>
  <KeepFormulaAfterRefresh>false</KeepFormulaAfterRefresh>
  <LocalAndCustomMemberRecognition>false</LocalAndCustomMemberRecognition>
  <LocalMemberAsCellPosition>false</LocalMemberAsCellPosition>
  <MeasureDisplayFormat>false</MeasureDisplayFormat>
  <NumberFormat>0.##</NumberFormat>
  <OnTheFlyMemberRecognition>false</OnTheFlyMemberRecognition>
  <OverrideEmptyValue>false</OverrideEmptyValue>
  <PerformRefreshSheetOnExpandCollapse>false</PerformRefreshSheetOnExpandCollapse>
  <RepeatColumnHeaders>false</RepeatColumnHeaders>
  <RepeatRowHeaders>false</RepeatRowHeaders>
```

Figure 6.3: Modifying the EPMXLClientPreferenceXML file

The sole purpose of this file is to set the initial behavior of the EPM Ribbon. It contains the default values for specific options and can be changed at any time.

Some clients prefer to push this file to the users' desktop to enable or disable certain features. Simplicity is most often the best approach when designing a user experience. Removing clutter from an interface, whether it is from a web page or an Excel template, is beneficial to avoid end user confusion and improve overall user adoption.

6.2 Summary

In this chapter readers learned how to customize and extend the add-in to get features beyond the ones that come out of the box. To illustrate these features, we talked about basic elements and concepts that are required to develop custom extensions using VBA, or by changing the underlying XML files.

In addition, users explored how to set default settings to facilitate the work of the administrators when rolling out the EPM Add-in to large audiences in order to enable only key features. This will help to avoid confusion or to facilitate training requirements in some cases.

Even when this was just a simple use case, this example can be used as a foundation to develop complex extensions to tailor the EPM Ribbon according to a client's requirement.

7. Summary

In this book, we have explored the key features of the EPM Add-in. With this information, the reader is now able to identify pain points and best practices to deploy a state of the art solution.

Likewise, we leveraged inside knowledge from the industry to explain the origins of some of the features and components that have been carried over with the acquisitions made by SAP over the past seven years.

In addition, we explored the latest functionality, which is available in the EPM Add-in 10.0 Service Pack 18, from a technically and a functional point of view.

By using a business case to depict a SAP Business Planning and Consolidation implementation in Rosie's Lemonade Company, we expect that the reader has developed a solid understanding of the core concepts within each module of the EPM Add-in. To illustrate each case, as mentioned in several chapters throughout the book, Rosie's requirements were taken from real life scenarios.

As demonstrated in each chapter, we have made every effort to keep this book very practical so that any end user can take advantage of the content that was created for this book.

Our newsletter will inform you about new publications and exclusive free downloads.

Subscribe today:

http://newsletter.espresso-tutorials.com

A About the Authors

Kermit Bravo is a Consultant at TruQua Enterprises, LLC, and offers deep techno-functional savvy in SAP, Banking, and Finance. Kermit started his career at IBM as a Project Management Financial Analyst before moving into a SAP FICO consultant position within the organization. For four years, he worked designing and developing financial solutions to help deliver value to customers. He left IBM in 2014 to join TruQua Enterprises as a BPC Consultant. While at IBM, Kermit specialized in FICO and in SAP Business Planning and Consolidation. He has a Masters in Finance with the Instituto Tecnológico de Monterrey in Mexico and a Masters in Banking from the University of Pompeu Fabra in Barcelona.

Scott Cairncross is a partner and co-founder of TruQua Enterprises, LLC. TruQua is an SAP software and services partner specializing in solving complex analytical problems within the enterprise. Scott is an expert in cross-industry planning and financial consolidation processes with deep product knowledge of SAP BPC (both Microsoft and SAP NetWeaver versions), SAP HANA, SAP BW and SAP BusinessObjects. He also specializes in user experience design and cloud-based developments and deployments. Scott has a proven track record in software development and project delivery of SAP solutions that are high-performing, provide long term customer value, reduce traditional SAP implementation costs, and lower total cost of maintenance. With project charters to improve both management effectiveness and operational efficiency, Scott has been through many full-life-cycle implementations at Fortune 100 companies. Scott has spoken regularly over the past decade at various events focusing on optimizing enterprise performance management such as SAP Insider, SAPPHIRE, ASUG, SAP d-Code (formerly TechEd) and others.

B Index

C Disclaimer

Names used in this book, trade names, commodity names etc. can be brands even though they have no marking and as such are subject to legal requirements.

All screenshots printed in this book are subject to copyright of SAP AG, Dietmar-Hopp-Allee 16, 69190 Walldorf, Germany.

This publication makes reference to products of SAP AG. SAP, R/3, SAP NetWeaver, Duet, PartnerEdge, ByDesign, SAP BusinessObjects Explorer, StreamWork, and other SAP products and services mentioned in the text, as well as the respective logos, are trademarks or registered trademarks of SAP AG in Germany and in other countries worldwide. Business Objects and the BusinessObjects logo, BusinessObjects, Crystal Reports, Crystal Decisions, Web Intelligence, Xcelsius, and other Business Objects products and services mentioned in the text as well as the respective logos are trademarks or registered trademarks of Business Objects Software Ltd. Business Objects is a company in the SAP AG group. Sybase and Adaptive Server, iAnywhere, Sybase 365, SQL Anywhere, and other Sybase products and services mentioned in the text as well as the respective logos are trademarks or registered trademarks of Sybase Inc. Sybase is a company in the SAP AG group. All other names of products and services are trademarks of the respective companies. The details in the text are not binding and are for information purposes only. Products may differ from country to country.

SAP Group shall not be liable for errors or omissions in this publication. The only warranties for SAP Group products and services are those that are set forth in the express warranty statements accompanying such products and services, if any. No further liability arises from the information contained in this publication.

More Espresso Tutorials Books

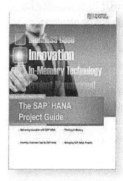

Ingo Brenckmann & Mathias Pöhling:

The SAP® HANA Project Guide

- ▶ Delivering innovation with SAP HANA
- ▶ Creating a business case for SAP HANA
- ▶ Thinking in-memory
- ▶ Managing SAP HANA projects

http://5009.espresso-tutorials.com

Martin Munzel:

New SAP® Controlling Planning Interface

- ▶ Introduction to Netweaver Business Client
- ▶ Flexible Planning Layouts
- ▶ Plan Data Upload from Excel

http://5011.espresso-tutorials.com

Janet Salmon & Ulrich Schlüter:

SAP HANA® for ERP Financials

- ▶ SAP ERP functionality for investment controlling

- ▶ Concepts, roles and different scenarios

- ▶ Effective planning and reporting

http://5092.espresso-tutorials.com

Thomas Michael:

Reporting for SAP® Asset Accounting

- ▶ Basic Asset Accounting Reporting Features

- ▶ Asset History Sheet

- ▶ Balance Reports

- ▶ Transaction Reports

http://5029.espresso-tutorials.com

Anurag Barua:

First Steps in SAP® Crystal Reports for Business Users

- ▶ Basic End-User Navigation
- ▶ Step-by-Step Business Reporting Scenario
- ▶ Best Practices for Report Distribution

http://5017.espresso-tutorials.com

Coleen Bedrosian:

Six Sigma Implementation Guide

- ▶ Six Sigma and Lean Six Sigma Concepts
- ▶ The Impact on an SAP Implementation
- ▶ Sustainability and Continued Growth

http://5024.espresso-tutorials.com

Darren Hague:

Universal Worklist with SAP Netweaver® Portal

- ▶ Learn to Easily Execute Business Tasks Using Universal Worklist

- ▶ Expert Insights to Configure UWL Functionality

- ▶ Learn how to Include 3rd Party Worksflows

http://5076.espresso-tutorials.com

Michal Krawczyk:

SAP® SOA Integration – Enterprise Service Monitoring

- ▶ Tools for Monitoring SOA Scenarios

- ▶ SAP Application Interface Framework (AIF) Customization Best Practices

- ▶ Forward Error Handling and Error Conflict Handler Configuration Tips

http://5077.espresso-tutorials.com